"*Jayshree Seth serves as an outstanding role model for aspiring scientists and engineers, and The Heart of Science is a must-read that charts a path for those looking to explore meaningful thought leadership, science advocacy, or a fresh perspective on STEM careers.*"

— **Scott Kelly,** Engineer, Naval Aviator, former NASA Astronaut, and retired US Navy Captain

"*In addition to being a world-class scientist and engineer, Jayshree Seth is a world-class communicator, and The Heart of Science is a joy and an inspiration to read. Whether you're an engineer, work with engineers, a leader in a science-based organization or are simply curious about STEM, this book is not to be missed.*"

— **David Epstein,** Best-Selling Author of *Range*

"*Jayshree Seth demonstrates that her success in science and engineering innovation relies on her understanding of people and systems, and that "intrapreneurs", self-appointed innovation leaders on the inside of established organizations, are at the heart of innovative change. The Heart of Science shows us the power and creativity of STEM mindsets, especially when placed in the necessary human context.*"

— **Simone Ahuja,** Best-Selling Author of *Jugaad Innovation* and *Disrupt-It-Yourself*

"*Jayshree Seth thoughtfully blends her fresh perspective and science sensibilities with a memorable style to give readers a roadmap for navigating life, work, and legacy. Look no further for thought provoking frameworks and vital reminders of the impact that STEM advocacy will have on our world. I will read, reflect and return to The Heart of Science often!*"

— **Amy Aines,** Co-Author of *Championing Science*

"*The Heart of Science amplifies the call to bring the magic of problem-solving to the issues that stir the passions of future generations. In each article, Jayshree Seth leverages her unique role as a scientist and a science advocate to give voice to the issues surrounding the future of STEM in society. Her style is engineered to inform, influence, and inspire!*"

— **Rachel Hutter,** Senior Vice President Health & Engineering, The Walt Disney Company

"*I know Jayshree as a scientist, a leader, an advisor, and an advocate for positive change. Throughout The Heart of Science, she embodies our "3M Science. Applied to Life" platform, using her voice to elevate the role of science and engineering, connecting us all to broader themes that deserve consideration and action. We are lucky at 3M to benefit from her talents, skills, and dedication. I encourage readers from all walks of life to connect with her ideas and passion through the pages of this book, I certainly have.*"

— **Mike Roman,** 3M Chairman and Chief Executive Officer

THE HEART OF SCIENCE

ENGINEERING
FOOTPRINTS,
FINGERPRINTS,
& IMPRINTS

JAYSHREE SETH, PH.D.

First paperback edition, November 2020

ISBN: 978-0-578-78512-7 (paperback)
ISBN: 978-0-578-78513-4 (eBook)
Library of Congress Control Number: 2020920790

Editing by Eli Trybula
Book design by David James Group, Oakbrook Terrace, IL
Cover illustration by Cheryl Peaslee, Warrenville, IL
Advised by Sharon Jenkins and MC Writing Services, Houston, TX
Reviewed by Bridget Tully, Hampshire, IL

Published by the Society of Women Engineers
1300 East Randolph Street, Suite 3500, Chicago, IL
+1 (312) 596-5223 | www.swe.org

All proceeds of this book go to the
Jayshree Seth Scholarship for Women of Color in STEM
to be administered by the Society of Women Engineers.
The scholarship is aimed at helping underrepresented
minorities advance in STEM education and professions
related to engineering and technology.

CONTENTS

Foreword   X

Introduction   XIV

SECTION ONE

STATE OF SCIENCE   18

Science Advocacy: As Easy as A-B-C?!   22

Action for Science Advocacy: Light the Way!   26

The State of Science 2020: The Year to STEM Skepticism?   29

Health is Wealth: Is Science the New Currency?   32

Breaking the Genius Myth: Science Needs You!   35

Left-brain? Right-brain?   38
There's No Wrong-Brain-Right-Brain When It Comes to Science!

Set Your Mind, Make it Happen! Three Ways to Adopt a Maker Mindset   41

Eureka! Where Do Ideas Come From?   44

Five Ways You Can Give Your VOICE to STEM: 47
Sponsors, Teachers, Enthusiasts, and Mentors!

SECTION TWO

SHTEM   52

What's the Real Shtick? It's SHTEM!   56

Back to School Extra: The Art of Science Encouragement at Home   60

Curiosity   64

AT HOME with Science!   66

Summer Learning Laws!   69
Friends and Family, Unstructured Time, and New Experiences...

Virtually, a Summer of Learning...   71

Raising Innovation: The Six Most Common ERRORS!   76

The STEAM Engine That Could!   80
Overcoming the Problem of Female Underrepresentation

Raising Influence in Science and Engineering: RISE and Shine!   84

#GenerationEquality   88

SECTION THREE

LEADERSHIP   90

The Five Views of Leadership: What's in Your Scope?   94

Of Leaders and Ladders: Can You Lead Without Being "The Boss"?   97

Move Over SMART Goals, I'm SUPER Smart...!   100

Three Simple Ways Managers Can Sweeten the   102
     Relationship with Employees: And It's Not About Candy Coating!

The One-Word Secret to Giving Good TALKS...!   105

Time Management Giving You a Hard Time?   107

Range! The "IT Factor" for Innovation?   110

LEAD In the Twilight Zone! Between Reflection and Resolution...   113

Work that 2020 Vision: Light! Camera! Action!   117

PRACTICE: Exercising That Leadership Muscle   120

SECTION FOUR

THOUGHT LEADERSHIP   126

SUCCESS... In the Time of Pandemic   128

Got CHANGE? Penny for Your Thoughts...   131

Race to Cure: Going Antiviral...   136

WorldSkills! SKILLS for the Future World?   144

Confidence Rap   147

Minding the Confidence Gap? It's a Rap!   148

One Simple Tip for that "Work-Life Balance" Resolution!   154

Graduation! Of Thinking-Caps, Town-Gown Relationships   157
     and Degrees of Difficulty...

Making the List? Of Footprints, Fingerprints, and Imprints...   159

Acknowledgments   166

Bibliography   167

FOREWORD

Although I met her for the first time in 2019, in the last few years, I have had a front row seat to Dr. Seth's advocacy and her contributions. Not only has she used her podium to advance science, but also to advance access and representation in STEM professions. To give you a small idea of what it is like to work with Jayshree, when we reached out to do a podcast with her covering topics relevant to the pandemic as well as social justice she offered to compile her insights into a collection that would support women and underrepresented minorities not only in word but also in deed. I am very pleased to let readers know that all proceeds of this book will contribute towards the Jayshree Seth Scholarship for Women of Color in STEM. Awarded annually, this scholarship will support a woman pursing an undergraduate or graduate degree in a STEM field.

As I reflect on *The Heart of Science*, I think about how Jayshree has engineered her life and career, the details of which she provides throughout this collection. I consider how she offers her experiences, guiding us with her footprints along a trail that she blazed in many places. She spends the first part of this book walking us through the State of Science by summarizing her experiences and the major findings of the 3M State of Science Index, a global survey of public perception on the role and value of science. She brings us along on her travels, from the A-B-Cs of science advocacy to the value of a maker mindset, debunking neuromyths to empower us as we go. This path reveals the importance of context and interdisciplinary perspectives as she promotes SHTEM (Science, Humanities, Technology, Engineering, and Mathematics) in the second section. As a generalist and parent, she highlights the value of mentors, parents, and community.

From this, I see just how Jayshree has shaped innovation to touch lives. Her fingerprints reside across the surface of countless projects that range from empathetic innovations that give comfort to the smallest humans, all the way to sustainable advances such as the elimination of solvents in large-scale manufacturing processes. She embodies the concept of leading from one's "own rung of the ladder", offering pragmatic as well as conceptual advice for early- and mid-career professionals as well as undergraduate and graduate students considering a STEM career.

Above all, as I read through this body of work, I see the arc of the work-life semblance she advocates in the book's final section. Among the pieces of thought leadership she has provided, we begin to see the imprint of her contributions and legacy. I think of this book as a guide and friend, and whether you enjoy it from start to finish or cherry pick articles that interest you most, there is something within for each of us on our SHTEM journeys. These articles offer a moment to the busy professional looking for a breath of inspiration, or the graduate student reading group reflecting together on points to ponder. Each article stands on its own, while collectively revealing the value and character of a life in STEM.

We are excited to recognize her with our highest honor, the Society of Women Engineers' Achievement Award at WE20 which is also a fitting time to launch her book. I am certain it will inspire others just like it inspires me.

— **Karen Horting**
Executive Director & CEO, Society of Women Engineers
October 2020

INTRODUCTION

While growing up, I never thought of myself as the "science and engineering type". I knew I wanted to help people, improve lives, and make the world a better place. It was no surprise that I gravitated towards fields where this contextual pull is strong. I didn't associate science and engineering with such goals. I saw this missed connection in my daughter's attitudes too. Coincidentally, I learned this as a parent at the same time that I was learning professionally how the world views and values science. Based on the research that is out there, it's pretty typical for young girls to have communal interests without understanding how science, technology, engineering, and mathematics (STEM) could contribute towards their aspirations.

So, how in the world did I end up with a 27-year career in STEM, enjoying my role as Chief Science Advocate? Fortunately, I had very strong parental guidance that directed me to the field of engineering, and I had a willingness to follow the path laid out before me and give my best. When people read about my accomplishments, it typically surprises them to hear about my educational journey. I didn't get into the prestigious engineering institute in my hometown, Roorkee, India. I grew up on that campus; my dad, a Ph.D. in civil engineering, was on the faculty there and my brother did his engineering studies there as well. The institution's reputation was a source of local pride, and it was commonly understood that future enrollment was the desire of every child, or at least that of their parents. It's thanks to my progressive parents that, upon not securing admission there, I ended up at the Regional Engineering College in Trichy (now the National Institute of Technology), thousands of miles from home in another part of India. I say progressive, because at that time, I was one of the very few girls who not only left home but left to pursue an engineering education.

To make a long story short, my undergraduate degree lead to a master's program in the United States at Clarkson University in Potsdam, New York. At that point in my academic growth, it didn't matter to me that I was the only woman in our lab, as I had become accustomed to accepting that I was in a largely male-centric field. By that time, I think I had already accepted, deep down, that I was blazing a trail in many ways.

What I did encounter with my thesis research was a strong sense of what I now know is something many women and underrepresented minorities in STEM often feel. It is this feeling that, "Am I doing what I thought I wanted to be doing?" For years, I looked for a term to describe this experience, thinking, *somebody has to have looked into this,* and then I found the concept of communal goal incongruity in psychology.* When you feel communal goal incongruity, you tend to reevaluate what you are doing and how you could or should change it. Essentially, your work is missing something; it doesn't seem to excite or inspire you. At that time, it was only a sense of commitment, tied to my work ethic, that allowed me to continue and successfully complete the given project.

So, when it came time to make a decision to continue towards a Ph.D. in the same area, I made the scary decision to switch fields. I knew I would be starting over in some ways, but I was more inspired by the research topic compared to my ongoing work. Well, I was not inspired necessarily by the topic itself, but for the context I could build around it. Intuitively, what I ended up doing was pulling together information and building context around things myself to be able to say, "What I am doing *is* helping others." This context has not traditionally been easily available in STEM. I believe it was precisely my creative, arts, and humanities mindsets that allowed me to build that much-needed context, as well as communicate it effectively. As a result, it became something communal because I was able to inspire myself, inform others, and influence them to work jointly on endeavors to find success. Fortunately, I had an amazing advisor and very collaborative lab mates who understood my vision and supported me along the way.

I got a job offer from 3M after a successful summer internship there, and it happened to be in a completely different area from my doctoral work. Though I wasn't aware that I would be moving closer towards goal congruity, I knew instinctively that my communal mindset would guide me to learn, grow, and contribute. I accepted the job, not really appreciating how fortunate I was to end up in a culture of innovation at 3M where empowerment and collaboration were embedded in the systems, integrated in the processes, and woven into the cultural fabric itself. I had wonderful peers and amazing bosses who shaped me and were willing to be shaped by me. I realized that I may not have had a specific expertise, but I had the knack for identifying the problems to solve, developing context around them, and then innovatively solving them with tenacity.

What I learned along the way was that I could bring the context building and the communal mindset with me wherever I went, and it would be a cornerstone to my success. Of course, there were other requirements. If you want to be successful, you have to work hard and be resilient. More importantly though, what I thought was strange about myself has turned out to be what has served me most as an engineer, whether that was a diversity of thought and creativity of solutions or the interest in solving problems to improve lives.

---

*Diekman and Steinberg, 2013. "Navigating Social Roles in Pursuit of Important Goals: A Communal Goal Congruity Account of STEM Pursuits," Social and Personality Psychology Compass.

In my role as 3M's first ever Chief Science Advocate, I take this message wherever I go. Everyone *can* be the science and engineering type. Don't let pervasive stereotypes deter you. There is no single experience of what science is, what scientists do, and who enters, persists, and excels in science. I am a living example. We need diversity of thought and experiences to solve the problems we face as humanity. We need to provide that communal context to STEM fields and careers.

Everyone's journey in these fields will be unique, centered around their technical proficiency and anchored by their specific roles. For that reason, this book does not detail my technical work or the scientific explorations and product inventions. Instead, I draw upon the work of others that enhanced my own learning and provided me rich context to develop easy, memorable ways to incorporate leadership into my own vocabulary, thoughts, and actions. I have cited most of the work that influenced my thinking and encourage readers to dig deeper. This book is a collection of some of my experiences along my journey, as an engineer but also as a parent, as a science advocate and as a thought leader.

I compiled this book for young dreamers and changers who want to solve real problems that matter in the world. We need more people with communal goals and aspirations in STEM than ever before to meet the sustainability challenges we have ahead of us. To all the girls who want to change the world, this is for you. To all young folks, especially women, who wonder if they should consider STEM or leave STEM because humanities may feel more intuitive, this is for you. I have given you my *schpiel*, and mark my words, the real *shtick* is SHTEM (Science, Humanities, Technology, Engineering, and Math). We need you to bring that much needed mindset. For all the professional women in STEM, or those poised to start, wondering if they can succeed in a corporate career, this is for you. Let me tell you, you can change the rubrics, you must alter the metrics, and you will transform the optics.

I encourage you to find the expression of your communal mindset, or what I like to describe as the art of applying science to life. Follow your heart. Find your purpose. Build context to inform, influence, and inspire yourself and those around you, and then collaborate with others to creatively solve problems.

Be good. Work hard. Live well.

SECTION

State of Science
On the Need for STEM Advocacy

"We live in a society exquisitely dependent on science and technology, in which hardly anyone knows anything about science and technology."

— Carl Sagan, American Astronomer, Author, and Science Communicator

Science Advocacy:
As Easy as A-B-C?

Have you ever been surprised to learn that something isn't exactly how it seems? Our experiences and education frequently dictate how we view the world, but sometimes we just don't know what we don't know! When I was in elementary school, my teacher asked if anyone's father was a doctor and I raised my hand. I later told my mother about this and she explained that my father was indeed a "doctor", but not the kind that practices medicine. I was perplexed. She went on to say that my father's Ph.D. made him a "Doctor of Science". As a child, I figured that instead of fixing people, he fixed science. It wasn't until many years later that I truly understood the depth of his profession. Now, here I am, a "doctor" myself, working at a science-based company for almost three decades.

THE GLOBAL STATE OF SCIENCE

One of the things I value most after working as a scientist at 3M is its culture of empowerment. We are empowered to use science to improve lives. Science is one of our most distinguishing characteristics; it ties our business together and provides a foundational strength and passion for our work. Science matters to us. Because we value science, we wanted to understand what the world thought about the topic. In 2017, 3M initiated a series of surveys to track public attitudes towards science around the world, which we called the State of Science Index. This Index, or what I'll refer to as 3M SOSI throughout this book, uncovered many surprises about how people view science. The first survey was released publicly in 2018, and we have continued to learn from 3M SOSI each year.

In 2018, the most shocking initial revelation was this: 38% of respondents, nearly 4 in 10 people, said if science didn't exist their lives wouldn't be any different! This was one of the primary perceptions we've tried to overcome. This first year's data also revealed a stark disconnect: the expectations of science are high. While people didn't seem to appreciate science in their daily lives, 35% believed we could live on Mars in our lifetime. Despite people not caring about the role of science in their daily lives, 82% of people said they would encourage kids to pursue a career in science. Sounds like a classic case of "do as I say, not as I do". The dissonance within these results indicates that there's plenty of work to be done. Until I saw the results of 3M SOSI, I really didn't appreciate the fact that science does need *fixing*!

INFLUENCE TO ADVOCACY

When we launched 3M SOSI, we knew we needed to bolster science, technology, engineering and math (STEM) appreciation on a global scale, and I was appointed as 3M's first ever Chief Science Advocate in 2018. I've had the privilege to participate in some wonderful events and fascinating programs, meeting and learning from amazing scientists, educators, and students along the way.

Early in my role, I had the unique opportunity to talk with Captain Scott Kelly to discuss his non-traditional educational journey and how he believes we can inspire young minds. You see, he wasn't a great student growing up, and he will be the first to tell you that he was unmotivated as teenager. Serendipitously, at age 18, he found a copy of *The Right Stuff*, a book by Tom Wolfe about American pilots and astronauts, NASA's space program, and the research that developed rocket-powered aircraft. As he describes it, that moment inspired him to travel to space, which he did 18 years later. Captain Kelly talks about the necessity of inspiration and the obstacle of the genius-myth as we consider how to connect current students with the passions they may pursue in STEM careers.

It is always inspiring to meet enthusiastic students. I have been able to witness their accomplishments during my travels or when they visit 3M to participate in events such as the Disruptive Design Challenge, Young Scientist Challenge, and other STEM programs. 3M scientists serve as mentors in many of these programs and help to answer questions, supporting students as they navigate through their projects while also providing exposure to what STEM careers can entail. These interactions and experiences solidified, in my mind, the value of sponsorship and mentorship.

Over the last few years, I have spoken with numerous publications, appeared on podcasts, and conducted interviews across media outlets around the world to convey the challenges we're facing at societal levels about the lack of scientific awareness, while communicating possible solutions to this issue. I have emphasized the importance of making science relatable and giving it a human context. I have also shared my own education and career journey as well as experiences as a parent of a son and a daughter. Overwhelmingly, I have encountered receptive audiences who are excited to consider a future in which the public embraces the value of science while understanding its respective contributions, opportunities, and limitations.

COMMON LANGUAGE

My many trips, travelling to a total of 15 countries around the world, have allowed me to interact, not just with fellow 3Mers in those countries, but leaders from industry, academia, government, and more. In each environment, in my role as science advocate, I have encountered tremendous interest, not only in the results of 3M SOSI, but also in the 3M culture of innovation. As I interacted with leadership teams from various science-based organizations, it has become evident that leaders set the tone for organizational culture and its key elements.

At a personal level, as I traveled to other countries, I was also struck by how much we all have in common. We all wish to contribute to society and yearn to be inspired. I feel fortunate to have experienced these commonalities, which emerged when my colleagues and I took time to really get to know one another and connect with each other's work, using science to drive innovation.

Through all of this, I also learned that science needs champions of all kinds, including those who are trained in STEM careers and those beyond our industry. Advocacy is rooted in acknowledging facts, developing solutions, and changing the status quo. No matter your background, you can help others understand the impact of science in their lives.

IT'S AS EASY AS A-B-C

Acknowledge, be aware, and appreciate science

We have to move people away from scientific apathy. If people don't appreciate science in their everyday lives, it can have negative consequences for the future. Don't shrug off science in conversation or let others dismiss it as too complicated.

Break down barriers, boundaries, and biases

There are stereotypes and behaviors that make science less attractive to underrepresented minorities. Diversity and inclusion form a key pillar in scientific inquiry that unlocks the secrets to a sustainable future. Representation also matters for those who seek role models.

Communicate and champion science in a concise way

Science communication doesn't have to focus on the *what*, we need to start with the *why*. Science needs to be communicated within a context that is important to people, connecting science outcomes with how science improves lives. We need to bring people along with advancement rather than talking down to them.

Communicating science, and the scientific method, in a way that is relatable to those outside our realm inspires more people to ask, "What if?" This inspiration encourages real-world problem solving. It's imperative that we appreciate and celebrate the many scientific innovations, from the seemingly mundane to the once-in-a-lifetime, and the people behind it all. It is important that this connection encourages the next generation to pursue STEM careers, enabling aspirations that improve lives by contributing to scientific advances and innovation.

POINTS TO PONDER

Why do you think science is under-appreciated and taken-for-granted?

What are some ways we can all become more effective advocates to raise the profile of science?

Action for Science Advocacy:
Light the Way!

When she was younger, one of my daughter's chores was to pick up pinecones in the yard. In an attempt to avoid the chore, my daughter wanted to know why grass didn't grow under pine trees in our neighborhood. In her mind, grass under pine trees would hide the pinecones and she wouldn't have to pick them up. We used this as an opportunity to explore together why it is that grass does not grow under pine trees. (We learned that the soil is rendered acidic due to the decomposition of pine needles to inhibit the growth of other plants, a process called allelopathy.) It gave us an opportunity to teach her how to use the scientific method to answer her question, and I created a meaningful narrative about how she could solve the problem in our own backyard. That relevance sparked her curiosity and prompted her to engage in key aspects of science, a project we eventually called *Greening Under the Evergreens*. In general, relevance is a key theme when discussing science with unengaged audiences. And that's just one of the insights 3M SOSI (State of Science Index) offered us in its first year.

NEW YEAR, NEW FINDINGS

We dug deeper with our second survey to follow up on the results from the first survey to ask, "Why?" For instance, one in three people are skeptical of science. The top reasons people said that they were skeptical included, "Too many conflicting opinions by scientists" (38%) and "I'm skeptical of things I don't understand" (29%), to name a few. Those points of view are pervasive in society.

But the 2019 3M SOSI survey also revealed that we have a great opportunity to address some of the barriers to science appreciation. The data shows how scientists are overwhelmingly seen as trusted sources, but that people want to hear results in language that's easy to understand. They want to know science in a more relatable way to their everyday lives. The 2019 data validated how effective communications are part of the solution to light the way.

The role of Chief Science Advocate allows me to champion science appreciation efforts. There are three specific areas I've identified that amplify science advocacy:

- Put the **spotlight** on the humans behind everyday innovations

  Scientists are seen as credible, but many people (58%) view them as elitist or, you could say, unapproachable. Highlighting the human factor will not only engage and inspire people but also improve the approachability problem of scientists, thereby improving the public perception of science. My colleagues at 3M and I took a first step at showing our true personalities and passions in a video series called "Beyond the beaker". Telling our stories personalized our work by including details about our families, routines, and hobbies, from ballroom dancing and ultimate frisbee to coffee and childcare. We opened ourselves up to let the world see that scientists and engineers are people, and I hope others do the same.

- Clearly **highlight** the connections to everyday life and make science relatable

  If more people can relate to science, it will drive interest. In 2019, 84% of 3M SOSI participants said that scientists should make science more relatable to their everyday lives. Our team developed a downloadable guide, "Scientists as storytellers", to help enhance how science communicators explain their work. I encourage all STEM professionals to review this guide with storytelling recommendations from an award-winning journalist, retired astronaut, respected academics, and more.

- Keep STEM initiatives in the **limelight** to encourage exposure and education

  Outside of funding, 26% of people surveyed think inadequate training and education for students is the biggest obstacle to the future of science. I was fortunate enough to grow up in a science-minded community, but access to STEM cannot be limited to a privileged population. We must actively promote equitable outcomes for under represented and underresourced students in STEM with time, resources, and attention. Such efforts empower kids by supporting STEM classroom projects to get more engaged with science and to consider the science track in school and future careers. I am proud of all the work 3M does on STEM equity as it relates to investing in education, encouraging, and engaging young minds.

GROUNDING

Why is science advocacy so important? Science has afforded us much of what we enjoy today from medicine to smartphones and everything in between. The 2019 3M SOSI revealed that only 20% of people stand up for science when debating its merits with others. That means that the majority of people are either uncomfortable with, or unaware of, the need to promote the benefits of the field. This can have serious consequences, not just in funding and support, but also the pipeline of diverse talent in STEM which is needed to address the problems we face. Advocacy is perhaps the most authentic way to change hearts and minds to engage and inspire with a message that resonates.

We need to take action in our communities, workplaces, and even our homes. And we need to be persistent because advocacy takes time to take root, grow, and bloom.

POINTS TO PONDER

What can we all do to make ourselves seem more approachable and accessible?

How can we improve everyday science communications to reach more people?

The State of Science 2020:
The Year to STEM Skepticism?

Since 2018, 3M has released the SOSI (State of Science Index) annually to
track public attitudes towards science through multi-country, original research.
In 2020, prompted by the phenomenon of the COVID-19 pandemic, we conducted
two surveys: we fielded the *Pre-Pandemic Survey* a few months before the pandemic
hit, followed by the *Pandemic Pulse* in July-August 2020, about six months into
the pandemic. We wanted to capture a snapshot of how science was perceived
against the backdrop of the COVID-19 outbreak.

The relationship we have with science certainly evolved during the 2020
pandemic. This became very clear as I absorbed insights from the *Pandemic Pulse*.
I found myself reflecting on the past three years of our global studies. In 2018, the
results of the first 3M SOSI, revealed that the world has a complicated relationship
with science. That was still true in 2020, but a shift occurred as people experienced,
first-hand, the vital role that science plays in our everyday lives. In 2020, science became
more relevant, more important, and more inherently interesting. As scientists took
center stage on news platforms, the world listened. Science had a moment in 2020.
The results of the *Pandemic Pulse* were indeed interesting, they allowed us to compare
and contrast findings to our pre-pandemic SOSI, and the years prior to
that. Science skepticism had grown each year since 3M SOSI had started, making
skepticism an undeniable trend. But that trend reversed itself during the pandemic:
the percentage of science skeptics dropped by seven points from the *Pre-Pandemic
Survey*, marking the first decline in three years.

UNITED STATE OF SCIENCE

Knowing that the image of science may have improved because of a global
health crisis was certainly no cause for celebration. Nevertheless, the context behind
results from the 2020 study suggested that as the pandemic took hold, people felt
connected to science in their everyday lives. This was felt around the globe, including
in the United States where skepticism for science reversed too. American skepticism
dropped a remarkable eight percentage points from before the pandemic.
They were also aligned in their trust in science and said overwhelmingly that they
believed we should "follow the science" to contain the spread of COVID-19 (90%).

Perhaps the most significant data spoke to the unity in this sentiment, showing that Americans, whatever side of the aisle they sat on, saw the most important priority for the world to be the cure for COVID-19, as well as for other ongoing diseases.

In such moments, when virtually all of humanity faces the same existential crisis and confronts the same fears, science serves as a great unifier to vanquish the threat. Opportunity emerges to seize the momentum and STEM the tide of science skepticism. Science, technology, engineering, and math drive real change. I see this at 3M every day. *The Pandemic Pulse* revealed that 79% of the world said science will make their lives better in the next ten years, up 7 points from our pre-pandemic survey.

STEM SKEPTICISM AROUND SCIENCE

Globally, health has always been the top challenge people want science to solve for. As I discuss later in this section, with healthcare, science gets personal in many ways. It is no surprise, perhaps, that COVID-19 made respondents more likely to agree that science plays a critical role in solving public health crises (78%), and 92% believed our actions should follow scientific evidence and advice to contain the spread of COVID-19. Our inherent interest in our health provides a way-in to attract people to science more generally. It also provides a strategy for building an ongoing, healthy relationship with the scientific process, which is dynamic and relies on new data, discussion, and ongoing debate.

Trust in science was up as skepticism declined. In the *Pandemic Pulse*, 89% of participants said that they trust science, up 4 points on the prior year. Those working in scientific fields were the most trusted (84%) source for scientific information. The *infodemic* during the pandemic may risk undermining that trust. While technology gives us access to scientific information, the world remains mostly skeptical of social media with only 27% of people indicating that they trust social media posts as a source of scientific information. Conversely, close to half of people (47%) said that they trust company websites. There's a clear opportunity for scientists and science-based companies to be visible, accessible, and active in their advocacy to bolster a foundation of public trust in science.

During the pandemic, people saw images of nature thriving as humans took a pause. So, it's not surprising outside of healthcare, environmental impact (67%) remained the top concern among people who agree that there are negative consequences to a world without science. Times of crisis are not the time to put sustainable solutions on the back burner, but rather to continue showing the critical role of science in solving sustainability challenges. It also gives context that attracts under-represented minorities to STEM that builds a sustainable talent pipeline given their higher affinity to communal and prosocial goals. Global citizens were more likely

(74%) to agree that, as a result of the pandemic, the world needs more people pursuing STEM related careers to benefit society's future.

There's a multiplier effect that exists when everyone comes together to solve common goals. The world was more likely to agree (77%) that science needs more funding due to the pandemic. Survey results showed that people mostly hold governments responsible for solving societal issues associated with health, sustainability, and STEM equity. But our findings also suggest that the most positive impact likely happens with the shared responsibility that exists when scientists, governments, business leaders, NGOs, academic institutions, and individuals pull together in pursuit of common goals. The future of science relies on the additive power of strong partnerships bolstering the STEM ecosystem for the greater good. It's not a zero-sum game.

Given the results of 3M SOSI 2020, we understand the following key relationships:

Science of Health for Health of Science

Technology and Sociology of Trust

Engineering of Sustainable Solutions

Mathematics of Equality and Accountability

The COVID-19 pandemic pulled into focus the importance of science and technology. People said that they were 73% more likely to agree, due to the pandemic, that a strong STEM education for students is crucial. Taking action to help future scientists reach their full potential has never been of more importance. In addition to collective action it also inspires me to continue my work as Chief Science Advocate. We can all take action.

POINTS TO PONDER

How was your relationship to science influenced in 2020?

What actions can you take to stem the tide of skepticism towards science?

Health is Wealth:
Is Science the New Currency?

As the 2020 3M SOSI (State of Science Index) made clear, most people associate science with advancements in health care as it highlights the science behind the advances that improve our daily lives in ways that few others can. Many remarkable health care innovations have been made. Thanks to science, many more are to happen in our lifetime.

The 2018 3M SOSI presciently taught us that 25% of people thought the health care industry would be most impacted by science in the next five years, which was the largest representation of all industries measured. However, people were less aware of everything science touches to improve their daily lives, as 38% of respondents in the same survey said if science didn't exist their lives wouldn't be any different! An appreciation for science and its role in a healthy lifestyle can start at a young age in unassuming ways.

CULTURE OF HEALTH

I grew up in India with a very strong healthy-living mindset woven into the cultural practices. I remember walking barefoot on dew-laden grass every morning because it was "good for our health". We avoided the sun in the afternoon because it was "not good for our health". We would practice our yoga poses, eat nuts, fresh fruits, green vegetables, and homemade balanced meals, all because it was good for us. Virtually every good practice was holistically tied back to health because it was important for success and well-being, then and in the future.

I became even more acutely aware of health matters when I was diagnosed with asthma as a young child. I had to give up dance because of repeated bouts which held up practice. My mother had wanted me to learn dance, something she couldn't do as a child. She found a classical Indian dance guru for me, *ghungroos* (ankle bells) were bought, and classes began. Unfortunately, there was no easy way to manage my asthma and my dance days were over just as they got started.

WEALTH OF INNOVATION

One of the most exciting parts of working at 3M has been the wide diversity of businesses we are in: industrial, health care, consumer, electronics, and transportation, to name a few. That diversity is coupled with the "15% Culture", in which a portion of a 3Mer's work time can be dedicated to projects that are exciting specifically to them. This empowers us to collaborate on ideas that may not be directly related to our own area, and makes for a very fulfilling experience. It all came full circle when I was invited to participate in a brainstorming session conducted by what used to be our drug delivery business. The outcome of this session turned out to be the commitment to work on an improved inhaler.

This certainly had special significance for me because of my family history and childhood experiences. But on a larger scale, this has critical importance given the rise in air pollution and population growth around the world. As cited in the 3M press release for this initiative, "an estimated 334 million people have asthma worldwide, and 65 million suffer from moderate to severe COPD [chronic obstructive pulmonary disease] – a number expected to rise 24 percent by 2034, making COPD the world's third leading cause of death."

I felt a deep connection to the progress of the Intelligent Control Inhaler project, as it gave me a unique opportunity to observe the integration of the digital and material world while working on a problem that was near and dear to my heart. Multiple teams initially worked concurrently to build out prototypes of their lead ideas and concepts. I got to observe the remarkable process of innovation with rich dialog, discussion, and debate to arrive at the best solution for the customer, the best hardware, and the best software with the most intuitive user-friendly design. It takes true collaboration between engineers from several disciplines, including chemists, materials experts, computer scientists, and design specialists to bring something like this together.

FUTURE HEALTH OF SCIENCE

Disease treatment is the number one global challenge that people around the world think science can help solve (75%), and I've seen it first-hand. Our intuitive, fully integrated inhaler could help improve lives by helping people take their medicine correctly. It is breath actuated and has on-screen prompts to guide patients through the process of using their inhaler. The integration enables self-care, in that it relays accurate information back to the patient which they can opt to share with providers or caregivers. Integration of the digital and material elements of the inhaler into a single, streamlined product revealed to me just one aspect of the amazing potential for STEM as it relates to health care.

It is imperative that we appreciate and acknowledge the many innovations, from the seemingly mundane to the major, to those that are already improving lives for many every day. The 2020 3M SOSI identified that 82% of people agree that a world without science has serious negative consequences, with the first being risk to human health.

It is important that we make the connection to science and encourage the next generation to pursue STEM careers with the tremendous potential to improve lives by contributing to scientific advances and innovation in health care.

My aging parents traveled from India in 2018 to watch my daughter perform at her Indian classical dance graduation after nine years of training. My mother brought her knee brace, my dad his inhaler, and I breathed easy...*Ommm*.

POINTS TO PONDER

What are some of the health care advances that people easily overlook or are underappreciated?

How can we more effectively use science and innovation in health care to advocate for science?

Breaking the Genius Myth:
Science Needs You!

When was the first time you came across a "genius"? Was it a family member, a classmate, or someone you saw on TV? What was it about this person that made you think that they were a genius? I first heard reference to the word genius when my brother, only five years old at the time, was selected by his teacher to visit the Jodrell Bank Observatory. I asked my mother why he was going to a bank and not to school. I wasn't old enough to realize that my brother had been identified as "gifted" and was going to visit a famous site for astrophysics. Apparently, you get to look at the stars if you are smart!

Later in school, after moving back to India, I became aware of the most well-known geniuses: Thomas Edison (the inventor), Albert Einstein (the physicist), and Leonardo da Vinci (the artist). I also remember being very impressed with two bright minds who were in the news at the time: Shakuntala Devi, who was a mathematical genius named in the *Guinness Book of World Records* for her outstanding ability as a "human calculator", and Vishwanathan Anand, a chess wizard who became the youngest Indian to achieve the title of International Master at the age of 15. Genius, at that point in my life, meant someone with an exceptional gift.

GENIUS BARRIER

I had the occasion to think about the nature of genius in a different context when 3M SOSI (State of Science Index) uncovered that 36% of people believed that they needed to be geniuses to have careers in science! The statistic shocked and worried me; such a misconception could deter people from entering STEM careers. The study also indicated that the genius stereotype is higher in emerging economies (44%) compared to developed ones (29%). This could have a drastic impact on economies' transitions to skilled labor if people primarily compare themselves to famous scientific role models.

As a society, we are facing many grand challenges, the solutions for which will certainly require STEM professionals with diverse backgrounds and experiences. We need to chip away at the perceived "genius barrier" to science careers, if for no other reason than because it is not true. This point was proven again when 3M invited discussion with experts who showed how the road to genius is paved with curiosity and persistence.

BREAKING IT DOWN

We partnered with Nobel Media for a series of panels as part of the Nobel Prize Inspiration Initiative (NPII).[1] These discussions were designed to inspire and engage participants to be even better problem solvers today and in the future. I joined 3M employees, as well as researchers and students in the community, to learn from Professor Mario Molina, who was best known for his role in uncovering the Antarctic ozone hole. What is crucial to know about Professor Molina's story is that he didn't set out to make such a big discovery. It was his interest and curiosity around the impact of chlorofluorocarbons (CFCs) that provided the basis for his research. Little did he know, his work would not only contribute to our understanding of atmospheric chemistry, but also have a profound impact on the global environment. He had no idea that he would be hailed as a genius one day.

The stories of countless scientists and engineers are consistent with Molina's experience. STEM fields often seem to publicize major breakthroughs or individual accomplishments. Because of this, everyday people might not think themselves capable of such "eureka!" moments, so they may opt out of a scientific career as an option. In reality, each big breakthrough is the culmination of countless small advances, trial and error, and teamwork. The pervasive myth of lone geniuses, who made their breakthroughs without any help from others, also deter people from science. Oftentimes in media, scientists are portrayed as men which may not inspire girls. *"If she can see it, she can be it,"* a tagline from the Geena Davis Institute, aims to break down barriers for girls in STEM and encourage more relatable role models. More women are needed to bring in diversity of thought and help us solve tough challenges. The mad, maverick, genius, or geek scientist stereotypes can also be a deterrent.

GENIUS MOMENT

In my own experience, studying science wasn't about sheer intelligence, but more about determination and diligence. Recovering from setbacks, such as when I didn't get into the hometown institute, and resilience, which I had to exhibit when I left home, also played a key role. And in the career journey, one can emulate the qualities of *genius thinking* by taking initiative to solve problems, asking thoughtful questions, and collaborating with others to find answers. Above all, a sense of curiosity and wonder, combined with inspiration to solve problems, goes a long way in the pursuit of a successful science-based career. We can all reach for the stars. You don't have to have an exceptional gift. You don't have to be a genius to offer genius insights.

---

[1]"Nobel Prize Inspiration Initiative," The Nobel Prize

3M SOSI creates as much hope as it does concern. As I've mentioned previously, 82% of people surveyed globally in 2018 would encourage kids to pursue a career in science. Maybe it's as simple as encouraging them to look *into* something as they are looking *at* it.

POINTS TO PONDER

What should we say to people who think they need to be a genius to have a science-based career?

How can we address this misconception and engage more people in pursuing STEM?

Left-brain? Right-brain?
There's No Wrong-Brain-Right-Brain When It Comes to Science!

During one of our many trips to Delhi, we visited a distant relative who was a painter. Growing up in a family where it was implicitly understood that science-based pursuits were ideal as a professional choice and arts made for great hobbies that served to round-off your personality, I was very intrigued at the prospect of meeting a painter in the family. I remember being mesmerized by her artwork and impressed when I learned that her paintings adorned the hallways of Delhi's Palam airport. She was deaf and mute, yet able to express herself beautifully though her art. There was some discussion on the ride back that when parts of your brain don't work, the other senses can be heightened. I remember being fascinated by the brain and its mysterious workings where different portions could adapt and compensate.

There's a good chance you learned about "left-brain" and "right-brain" thinking at an early age. This is the frequently debunked neuromyth,[2] or common misconception about brain research, that presumes that humans can only have strengths in analytical or creative endeavors. I first encountered the widespread notion of left-brain and right-brain thinking when I moved to the United States for graduate school in the early 1990's. I must admit, the concept puzzled me. The idea, that imaginative and intuitive people use the right part of their brain more while those who use the left side of their brain are somehow more logical and quantitative thinking, left me confused and uninspired.

A QUESTIONABLE MINDSET

So, why does it matter if people believe in neuromyths? To this day, when it comes to the topic of brain research, the takeaways are often oversimplifications that reduce complex issues to just one factor, such as "Right-brained kids can't excel in STEM subjects," or "Left-brained kids can't be creative." If students or adults internalize this neuromyth, it could impact their sense of self-efficacy,[3] which is the confidence they have in their ability to succeed. Research has shown that students' beliefs of self-efficacy predict their ability to succeed at an academic task. In other

---

[2] Robert H. Shmerling, "Right brain/left brain, right?" Harvard Health Blog, August 25, 2017.
[3] Kara Blacker, "Science of Adolescent Learning: Debunking the Myth about Left-Brain/Right-Brain Learning Styles," Alliance for Excellent Education, December 14, 2016.

words, if a student finds themselves being frequently labeled as "right-brained," their belief in its truth could negatively impact their performance and perception toward STEM-based topics.

On a related note, 3M SOSI (State of Science Index) found that more than 25% of adults worldwide do not see the point of needing to understand science as an adult. I wish I could dig deeper to learn more about the motivations behind those answers and find out how many of these people were perhaps told that they are "right-brain people".

GENIUS-THINKING

As a modern society, we certainly value engineering, medical, and scientific roles, perhaps so much that they seem inaccessible. As we just discussed, 3M SOSI found that 36% of people think only geniuses can have a career in science. Combine this with the infamous brain-side neuromyth, and you may have a recipe for avoiding STEM at all costs.

Simply put, because we know that there's no physical propensity for using just one side of your brain or the other, we should promote using both! Society needs creative scientists for continued innovation. And artists and creatives can benefit from knowing more about science and technology. Scientists usually don't have a reputation for being very creative. The notion that they have to adhere to the scientific method, generate copious amounts of data, and conduct tedious analysis of results, often suggests a lack of creativity. But few would dispute that the great scientific and technological innovators were creative thinkers. Science is, after all, a highly creative undertaking. "The greatest scientists are artists as well." Albert Einstein famously also said, "Imagination is more important than knowledge."

MOVING BEYOND THE CRANIUM

Brain activity has been described as a "neural concert", where individual players may have a stronger role during certain parts, but neither side of the orchestra dominates.[4] But, just like with a concert, practice makes better. The brain may be mysterious but it's a mental muscle, and one that can and should be stretched!

Here are a few *exercises* that can help children and adults move past the brain dominance paradigm:

---

[4]Bongard, Ferrandez, and Fernandez, 2009. "The neural concert of vision," Neurocomputing.

- **Strengthen** the imagination

  Practice the possibilities by training your mind to be curious. Create, visualize, and communicate new ways to solve problems. Think about the everyday challenges you experience in your daily life and how they can be improved.

- **Deepen** your appreciation of the detail

  Deliberate the practicalities by engaging in tasks that provide opportunity for strategic planning and goal setting. Learning to appreciate the details will give you a newfound appreciation for analytical pursuits.

- **Broaden** your knowledge-base and **widen** your network

  Foster uncommon connections, as creative inspiration can come from variety of sources, which are often unrelated. Get yourself out of your comfort zone and seek motivation from new destinations, new foods, new books, or new people.

As someone deeply engaged in R&D (research and development) for developing new-to-the-world products, I know that scientists can be both analytical and artistic. To be successful, scientists have to shift between divergent and convergent thinking constantly. It's not simply one or the other that's required. In my opinion, STEM leaders of the future have to be integrated thinkers who can balance and develop their creativity and analytical skills concurrently, not in spite of each other. Now that's a *no-brainer!*

3M SOSI also found that 20% of today's adults (ages 18-34) claim to know "a lot" about science versus 9% of adults 51 and older. This tells me that there's room for change. So, I encourage everyone to consider how can we combat negative stereotypes about right- or left-brained thinking to improve appreciation of science.

POINTS TO PONDER

How can we change the way we compliment kids to move us past traditional neuromyths?

What approaches expose new ways thinking and espouse the values of being multi-discipline thinkers?

Set Your Mind, Make it Happen!
Three Ways to Adopt a Maker Mindset

Have you ever crafted something with your own two hands? Do you remember the feeling of creating it from scratch and seeing it through to completion? Perhaps it was an inventive tool, a fun toy, or an artistic treasure that brought joy to your life. As a child, I transformed broken glass bangles with the flame of a candle into colorful necklaces and bracelets. I was so proud of my work, of what I had made. *Making* is innate to human behavior. As humans, we became who we are, largely, because we made things. Our tools have defined our evolution in many ways, and our survival on this planet was ensured because we learned to make what we need.

I remember a particularly meaningful project from a few years ago where I used small beads and glitter to create Indian motifs to give as gifts to many of my relatives. It took me a few weeks from start to finish, where I imagined, experimented, and completed these treasures. Instead of simply buying, I was able to present handmade gifts and felt a sense of accomplishment. My children watched as I tinkered, hopefully inspired by what they saw. After all, role modeling is important for children.

As a scientist by trade, I sought tools and techniques that could help me in creating unique designs. As an amateur artist, I realized how fun and rewarding it was. But, even if you aren't a scientist, artist, or craftsperson, there are ways to appreciate the practical value of making things to test your limits, be in a learning mode, and develop a growth mindset.

MAKING AN IMPACT

The 2018 3M SOSI (State of Science Index) taught us that 27% of adults worldwide do not see the need to understand science as an adult. That means over a quarter of people are disengaged from science and the scientific mindset. If adults lose interest in science, what message are they sending to the younger generation?

Thankfully, educators and hobbyists advocated for a "maker movement" that brings back a *maker mindset*. It's one way of iterating on ideas to solve problems and collaborate with peers to make those solutions real. The maker mindset is not just brainstorming ideas, but the profound experience of bringing ideas to life through hands-on experimentation and DIY (Do-It-Yourself) building. It ultimately involves a heightened sense of curiosity and wonder. After all, the maker mindset is consistent with many key elements of a scientific mindset that include embracing curiosity, experimentation, skepticism, and collaboration.

RETURN TO OUR ROOTS

As human beings, we have a scientific mindset built-in! It's especially present during early childhood when young kids hypothesize, test, and assess constantly without even realizing it. We became who we are as a species largely because we made things, experimented, and improvised, learning along the way. However, many times as we grow up, we tend to get conditioned to always have the right answers and never make mistakes. We often tell our children that it's okay to fail, yet many of us, as adults, are afraid of failure and unwilling to fail.

Thanks to the maker movement, many K-12 teachers have embraced classroom "maker spaces". These environments allow students to experiment with different supplies to build things and better understand the world around them. I'm hopeful that such spaces will help instill a scientific mindset and a lifelong appreciation for STEM subjects.

MAKE, BELIEVE

So, how can we have more people embrace a mindset that welcomes the process of challenging assumptions? How can we empower more people to create and get their hands dirty, trading immediate perfection for grit and resilience? Here are three tips adults can use to adopt more of a scientific and maker mindset even in the absence of a scientific career.

- **Treasure curiosity:** Remember to have fun with it!

    The idea of making something shouldn't feel like a chore or impossible task to perfect, it's a way to continually learn. Consider weekend hobbies which could challenge you to view your abilities differently. The only person you need to impress is yourself. If you're having fun and learning new concepts while crafting, writing, or building an object to solve a problem, it's a total win. Curiosity and a self-motivated pursuit of knowledge promotes an affinity towards critical thinking.

- **Tools are at your disposal:** Depict, devise, deliver...

    Investigate ways to solve common challenges you may have encountered in your daily life. Start by depicting the problem in words or pictures, devising a solution based on what tools you have around. Deliver a rudimentary prototype after minimal research on the internet. It could be as simple as a DIY solution, made with foam and tape, for drafty windows like we experience where I live in cold Minnesota. The main objective is to flex the creative muscles and experiment with ideas to make something with your own hands.

- **Toy with your beliefs:** Challenge your own biases

  A healthy dose of skepticism is essential for a scientific mindset because it challenges us to seek out more information to formulate a point of view. This allows us the chance to see problems and solutions from new perspectives. Think of a time where someone presented an alternative point of view. Did you try to validate it with research, or did you have a fixed mindset that was resistant to change? Remember that it's okay to not always be correct. Sometimes our life experiences impact how we view the world. We need to ask questions and consult and collaborate with others to be as effective and informed as possible.

A maker mindset *is* a growth mindset, a critical thinking mindset, a scientific mindset!

POINTS TO PONDER

How can we encourage the joy of making in young kids from all walks of life and link it to the scientific process?

How can we get more people to appreciate and link the value of tinkering to developing a scientific mindset?

Eureka!
Where Do Ideas Come From?

Do you remember the first time you had a big idea? Was it a game you made up? Perhaps it was a sci-fi futuristic invention you imagined that could solve some of your problems? Or was it a simple hack to help you do a mundane task? Ideas and inventions are the lifeblood of innovation. Any day is a good day to think about innovative ideas and creative thinking to improve lives and make the world a better place.

IDEAS START YOUNG

Most ideas come from trying to solve problems. I remember my first original *idea*. I was about four years old and watched my brother cry everyday as my mom tried to detangle and comb his extremely curly, long hair. After one such day, I had an idea: I grabbed a pair of scissors and cut off a few strands. My brother immediately ran to our mother clutching the hair in is hand, yelling, "She cut God's hair, she cut God's hair!" I was so scared that I still vividly remember hiding behind the sofa in the living room. My mother later explained to me the longstanding family tradition that the firstborn son's hair would be cut for the first time at a special ceremony after they turned five years old. It was sacred hair, if you will.

Let's just say my first idea didn't quite cut it. But it taught me that I was an action-oriented problem solver, with a desire for pushing boundaries! As a scientist, I love coming up with ideas to solve customer problems, develop new products and platforms, and apply science to improve lives. The inspiration for ideas can come from virtually anywhere.

In my mind, inspiration can come from focusing on internal strategic direction for innovation, customer feedback on concepts and prototypes, improvement opportunities for existing offerings, evolving market needs and trends, potential disruptions, and (of course) serendipity. But in all cases, the creation, implementation, and longevity of a given innovation is most effective when it is backed with good contextual information, sound customer insights, and rigorous science.

IT'S ALL GREEK TO ME!

When students learn that I hold over 50 patents, they regularly ask me, "Where do ideas come from?" I explain to them what I think are sources of inspiration for new inventions and products. In the midst of one such interaction with these young scientists, I had a "eureka moment". I put my understanding of inspiration in a context many scientists and engineers use: the Greek alphabet. So, what can inspire new ideas? I give you: Idea Greek!

- **Alpha** decisions

  Concentrate on the strategy laid out for the organization by high ranking leadership. That direction can allow you to focus creative energy to solve very specific, identified problem areas.

- **Beta** testing

  Evaluate the prototypes of new concepts with customers and seek feedback on features based on a minimally viable prototype.

- **Delta** assessment

  Establish the shortcomings of current products and find solutions to evolve with customer needs.

- **Theta** function

  Understand the unarticulated needs that can lead to disruptive ideas by finding the connections between complex customer variables, much like theta functions in math.

- **Sigma** factor

  Observe external factors, such as technology or business trends, that can create or change customer requirements, just like the sigma factor in gene transcription, which depends upon environmental conditions.

- **Psi** phenomenon

  Sometimes ideas can appear from nowhere, almost like paranormal factors or psychic abilities that cannot be explained. Gut and intuition do play a role, but "chance always favors a prepared mind."[5]

Then, there are always the **Pi**(e) in the sky, wild ideas. There is not an *iota* of doubt that the seemingly wild ideas of yesterday can be the most innovative ideas of today. No one has a monopoly on ideas because we are all creative. Sometimes we just need to recognize and unleash that power.

---

[5] Famously stated by Louis Pasteur

AT HOME WITH INNOVATION

I remember when I encouraged my, then middle-schooler, son to participate in the local Young Inventor Fair. His answer was, "But, I am not an inventor," and he went back to reading his book. His bookmark caught my eye, and "Book BOB" (Bunch Of Bookmarks) was born. Turns out, my son had trouble with paper bookmarks that would tear or fall out, so he had started using wool strands that he had tied together loosely. Every time he needed a bookmark, he would pull a strand out from the bunch. I pointed out to him, gently, that he had transformed a piece of string into a tool.

"So, I am an inventor?!" His realization was initiated by a simple observation, changing how he viewed himself. Once he solved a problem relevant to his life, he saw the value in everyday innovation and improvised solutions, or Jugaad Innovation, as it has been referred to, a nod to frugal innovation and ingenuity.[6]

My son was excited to make Book BOBs in many color combinations and sizes. He would place them on objects in his room such that they looked like a curly mop of hair on faces, pulling one out each time he started a new book. The best part? No scissors required! Consider "Idea Greek" to seek inspiration and jump-start your innovation machine.

POINTS TO PONDER

*What were some of your early ideas and
what problems were you trying to solve?*

*What additional sources of ideas can you think of
to add to the "Idea Greek" to jumpstart innovation?*

---

[6] Radjou, Prabhu, and Ahuja, Jugaad Innovation: Think Frugal, Be Flexible, Generate Breakthrough Growth.

Five Ways You Can Give Your VOICE to STEM:
Sponsors, Teachers, Enthusiasts, and Mentors!

These might seem like odd questions, but take a moment to consider: Could an 11-year-old develop a mobile app capable of detecting lead in water? Do you think a 13-year-old can treat pancreatic cancer with A.I. (artificial intelligence)? What does a 14-year-old know about replacing antibiotics with nanoparticle bandages to reduce the risk of super bugs? If you've heard about winners of the Discovery Education 3M Young Scientist Challenge, your answer would be an emphatic, "YES!"

I have had the chance to meet these young scientists in-person and learn about their winning projects. Not only do students demonstrate spot-on thinking, but their motivations are sincere. Through the support of 3M mentors, these students made substantive contributions by completing complex projects such as prototyping a nanotube sensor and mobile application capable of testing water for lead in real-time, testing the feasibility of algorithms in healthcare, and creating a kale and copper-based treatment that eliminates the need for antibiotics in wound care. Many 3Mers devote time to helping students reach a breakthrough because we want to help people of *all* ages appreciate science.

As I interacted with the participants of the Young Scientist Challenge, it was evident that their curiosity, imagination, and passion played a role in their success. But the critical role of strong support from parents, teachers, and the scientific community was evident as well. In other words, "it took a village" to raise these young scientists. The more I think about it, I realize that STEM is more than just a mashup of four disciplines, it also spells success for these students because of: **S**ponsors, **T**eachers, **E**nthusiasts, **M**entors. Each role plants the seeds of scientific appreciation in the next generation, nurtures them, and watches them grow into well-informed problem-solvers capable of navigating uncertainty and complexity.

STARTING EARLY AND OFTEN

Seeds for STEM need to be planted early. It has been well established that when parents are actively involved in schoolwork,[7] their children perform better in the classroom. The 2018 3M SOSI (State of Science Index) reveals that 92% of parents surveyed want their kids to know more about science and that the strong

---

[7] Rebecca Fraser-Thill, "Parent Involvement Can Benefit Children in Many Ways," verywell family, May 14, 2020.

majority would encourage kids to pursue a career in science. Some parents may have low self-confidence when it comes to STEM, and that may impact their child's attitude toward the disciplines. We've unpacked the neuromyths of genius and the way the brain works because 3M SOSI indicates that one-third of people believe that only geniuses can have a career in science. There seem to be many barriers to STEM education and careers; attitude is one we can address almost immediately. It's important to recognize that appreciating *and* knowing science shouldn't be conflated. Just like you don't have to be an artist to appreciate art, you don't have to be a scientist to appreciate science. In many ways, anyone in the community can value the role science plays and support those engaged in teaching and learning.

GIVING A VOICE TO SCIENCE FOR ALL

Normally, informal learning that happens in after-school clubs, museums, and libraries helps round out a child's education. Interactive exhibits and intuitive displays can go a long way towards instilling a sense of curiosity and a fun, shared experience in kids and parents alike. But what happens to the promising students who don't have access to these opportunities? Teachers and parents with limited resources need the help of supporters and enthusiasts to reinforce the value of STEM and increase its accessibility so that it is available to all, not only the elite or privileged few.

I've been involved in many science-based, kids' activities over the years and know first-hand the critical role **volunteers** play regardless of background. If you have a STEM background, you can volunteer as a mentor for projects and programs or explore speaking opportunities at schools. For example, 3M developed the Visiting Wizards program, designed to bring STEM-based fun to elementary and middle school classrooms at a teacher's request. Our scientists and engineers volunteer to conduct a demonstration, allowing them the chance to reconnect with their passion while offering a bit of awe to curious young minds.

Many communities lack the connections to facilitate events such as STEM career days. If you have a child in school, email their teacher and proactively ask if they need any specialists or help in **organizing** events. If you work for a company, ask the human resources and philanthropy teams about organizing mentorship programs with local non-profit organizations. This can include corporate matching to channel resources to increase opportunities.

Show kids how science solves problems! It's important to communicate how science works in a context that children see as important. Explain your day-to-day work life as a STEM professional, and don't forget to talk about the failures you've encountered. Acknowledging the ups and downs is important so that kids and adults know that it is part of the scientific process. This **inspires** resilience.

Make the case for science-based programs and funding in your community or through the company you work for. **Champion** to bring more STEM tools into your local schools and communities. Through corporate or civic involvement and advocacy, you can improve perceptions about science.

Let the ordinary seem extraordinary. **Engage** in conversations that draw out the natural curiosity and wonder that kids have in abundance so that you can engage in learning together. Discuss the things around you that might seem mundane, though they are anything but that!

Here are some ways we can make science more accessible, and a source of wonder, for everyone to enjoy. It's up to us to give our VOICE by:

Volunteering

Organizing

Inspiring

Championing

Engaging

In my role as Chief Science Advocate, I get the opportunity to meet with teachers, educators, and scientific leaders. I always thank them for the hard work they do. I want to express my gratitude to everyone who has and will continue to donate their time and resources, giving VOICE to science appreciation.

POINTS TO PONDER

How can we nurture the love for science and create minds filled with curiosity and wonder?

How can we help to bridge the gap between advantaged and disadvantaged students?

SECTION 2

SHTEM
On the Need for Convergence of STEM and Humanities

"Science is but persuasion of itself unless it has as its ultimate goal the betterment of humanity."

— Nikola Tesla, Serbian-American Inventor, Engineer, and Futurist

What's the Real Shtick?
It's SHTEM!

In just the first month of its publication, we shared the 2019 3M SOSI (State of Science Index) with thousands of people and discussed its results at various forums. That time allowed me to reflect and crystallize some more thoughts on effective and inclusive approaches to science advocacy. Among the survey's key findings, 87% of the global community believed we need science to solve the world's problems; however, skepticism of science grew, with nearly half the world (45%) stating they only believe in science that aligns with, and likely reinforces, their personal beliefs. In my view, the current state of science reinforces the importance of the humanities!

Tackling today's biggest scientific and technological challenges will require not just the ability to think critically, but also to be able to apply it within the human context. This is an ability that can be developed through learning which emphasizes STEM *and* key elements of humanities, which is functionally the study of human society and culture. There has been much discussion lately that, to have the impact that science can truly have, lessons in the humanities will be crucial. In many ways, STEM subjects focus on certainty and a quest for answers while the humanities focus on dealing with uncertainty and a drive for questions.[8] Where STEM seeks to analyze, the humanities can help to synthesize.

TRANSDISCIPLINARY DISCIPLINE

Many of the challenges we currently face cross disciplinary boundaries. Often, the most enduring and transformative innovations take place at the confluence of various disciplines. Seemingly, as more students opt for occupationally linked majors, transdisciplinary learning needs to be encouraged to appreciate the intrinsic value and impactful application of STEM. The ability to meaningfully engage, think critically, listen empathetically, and communicate and collaborate effectively can be enhanced with the humanities. Moreover, exposure to transdisciplinary topics, practitioners, and problems can bring in diversity of thought, thereby enhancing their effectiveness in comparison with monolithic groups.

Based on the experience with my own children, I also believe that a greater emphasis on highlighting the importance of the humanities in STEM fields could

---

[8] John Horgan, "Why STEM Students Need Humanities Courses," Scientific American, August 16, 2018.

attract and retain more girls and women, who often perceive STEM fields as "dry". *Context* is always critical in inspiring my daughter to pursue STEM projects whereas the content would suffice for my son. For many girls and women, the idea of an education and a career that has the capability to shape our world for the better, within the context of our society, is very inspiring as they often show a natural inclination towards the humanities.[9] In fact, the same inclination has been a critical factor in my own STEM career success.

FICTION OF F.A.C.T.

Perhaps the largest impact of humanities and social sciences can be in the area of science communication. There has been much research on the science of why we deny science in recent years.[10] People don't reject the field of science entirely. In fact, the 2019 3M SOSI reported that 85% of people surveyed said they want to know more about science. However, issues arise when they see something that conflicts with deeply held views. Researchers, such as Professor Dan Kahan at Yale and others, have in fact studied how what we choose to believe is tied in with our identities. With that being the case, it is imperative we adjust the narrative accordingly.

Humans apply the well-practiced fight-or-flight reflexes to data itself! Science shows that our strong reactions arise much faster than our ability to apply conscious thought. It is believed to be a necessary evolutionary process so we could react quickly to danger.[10] Given that insight, it is critical to present information with the right context to avoid eliciting an immediate defensive response. Also, we are more likely to heed evidence and arguments that bolster our beliefs, known as "confirmation bias", and oppose views and arguments that we find incongruent with our beliefs.[10] Knowing that people gravitate toward information that confirms what they know, it is clear that the way to persuade people is not via evidence and argument. Instead, it's about communicating the "value narrative", the empathetic storytelling that gets the message across to initiate interest and increase understanding.

Recent studies have found that people with more scientific curiosity were more likely to be open-minded about information that challenged their existing views.[11] Those who have an appetite to be surprised by scientific information react more open-mindedly. The key is to find ways to inculcate a scientifically curious mindset and the key is to foster its development at an early age. Many say they are skeptical of science and are becoming increasingly distrustful, but therein lies the "paradox of trust": you can't trust something until you understand it, but you can't understand something

---

[9] Clare McGrane, "Misconceptions and stereotypes may discourage girls from studying STEM, study finds," GeekWire, March 13, 2018.
[10] Chris Mooney, "The Science of Why We Don't Believe Science," Mother Jones, May/June 2011.
[11] Kahan et al., 2017. "Science Curiosity and Political Information Processing," Political Psychology.

without trusting it first. Human trust is a fluid concept and very personal at that.

It's a FACT that we need a better understanding of the public impact of science as well as a better understanding of what influences our willingness to engage with and trust it:

> **Fight or flight**
>
> **Affirmation versus accuracy**
>
> **Curious case of curiosity**
>
> **Trust and the paradox thereof**

THE SCHPIEL

The 2019 3M SOSI suggested that connecting the dots between science and its positive impact on humanity is an important driver of interest in and support for science. This information places specific emphasis on effective communication and humanization of science. Championing for science gets easier as people get excited when they understand how the work of scientists can change the world.[12]

I had the opportunity to consider how to provide the human context to my scientific endeavors while participating in a nationally televised brand campaign for 3M. We created the content through a series of interviews to produce three segments.

"Ideas that grow"
The first idea described what I love most about being a scientist at 3M: the fact that I am part of a community of problem solvers. I value how we develop everyday solutions while building upon ideas to take on bigger challenges. We are constantly innovating to bring new inspiration to solve problems that improve lives.

"People helping people"
We used the second segment to highlight the importance of empathy and how we are committed to helping other people. Throughout my career with 3M, the value of listening, observing, and understanding others' perspectives has been reinforced in ways that lead to meaningful solutions. Every invention is inspired by people, their needs, their hurdles, and their desire for a better solution.

"Scientific journey"
Our final segment underscored the hard work and dedication that goes into solving problems. Scientific discovery is not just about that one "a-ha" moment! It's about discipline and rigor in the scientific process to provide solutions that have to work.

---

[12] Aines and Aines, *Championing Science: Communicating Your Ideas to Decision Makers.*

A process that involves time, dedication, and a relentless pursuit of making things better and better.

I gave my *schpiel*,[13] the real *shtick* is SHTEM, it's the interaction of the Humanities with STEM! If the chasm between STEM and humanities widens, both disciplines have a lot to lose.

POINTS TO PONDER

What more can we do to bridge the gap between STEM and Humanities and increase science awareness and appreciation?

What humanities courses do you think would benefit a traditional STEM education?

---

[13] Yiddish words for short story (schpiel) and attribute, piece, or thing (shtick).

Back to School Extra:
The Art of Science Encouragement at Home

As you know by now, I grew up in a university town in India surrounded by scientists and engineers. If it weren't for that, I am fairly certain I would not have gone down that path. The same could be said for my peers who grew up in that environment but under different economic conditions or educational backgrounds. Interestingly enough, data from the 2018 and 2019 3M SOSIs show that India ranked highest for level of trust toward science among the countries surveyed. There is deep appreciation for STEM engrained in the culture, and it was this surrounding environment and strong parental guidance that led me to become an engineer. But not everyone has these opportunities. We can't underestimate the impact environmental factors can have on the careers children choose and the future they lead. Many people credit their parents, teachers, or community for the nudge down a certain career path.

SCIENCE INTEREST AT HOME

How can we, as parents, create an environment for more students to be interested in science at an early age even if we aren't regularly exposed to it? The 2018 3M SOSI also found an interesting disconnect that inspired this article: around the world, parents want their kids to know more about science, but more than one in four adults don't see the point in understanding science. Regardless of your comfort level, the scientific method is a great way to encourage kids to think about why or how things work. They simply need to ask a question about something they like, develop a hypothesis (why they think something happens), find ways to answer their question, and understand their findings. This can turn into a fun weekly game for the entire family.

If your kids are struggling with homework, try to support them in fun and creative ways. I would make little rhymes to help my kids memorize scientific concepts. They loved it and it created a sense of excitement and anticipation. This could be helpful for those who consider themselves creative or witty. Do you subscribe to online streaming services like Netflix or Hulu? Check out documentaries and science programming that encourage everyone in the family to learn together in the comfort of your living room. If learning feels like an activity, instead of a chore, it could intrigue kids.

SCIENCE AFTER THE BELL RINGS

Kids who are inspired by their "at home scientific method" can put it into practice at an after-school science club or program. Whether it's through their school or an extra-curricular program, science can inspire curiosity and wonder. Furthermore, many of these programs offer certifications or competitions that can prepare them for the future.

For many youngsters, seeing people in the community who have science-based careers could have a positive impact. The 2018 3M SOSI noted that 28% of parents think mentorship is an effective way to encourage a career in science. If you have any friends or family members that work in STEM fields, it might be interesting to meet them or setup a videocall so that your kids can ask questions about their daily work activities and responsibilities.

STRATEGIES FOR SUCCESS

If you put science into something relatable, like sports or cooking, it can help kids better understand the way things work. Believe it or not, cooking can be like a science experiment and your kitchen a science lab! My daughter's simple questions about bread-making led to her first science project win in middle school, titled Bread Dough D.O.E. (Design of Experiments). At the end of the day there is no exact recipe, but here are key strategies you can consider as a parent:

- Promote **exploration**

   Exploration leads to appreciating and learning about the science in our everyday lives. Museums, books, videos, programs, toys, and games are a great start.

- Facilitate **exposure**

   Exposure encourages listening and interacting with a diverse range of STEM professionals and others engaged in science-based careers. What do these jobs entail and how do they solve problems to make the world a better place?

- Encourage **experimentation**

   Experimentation provides opportunities for kids to be doing and experiencing, to observe, question, hypothesize, understand while getting their hands dirty...and developing a scientific thought process.

- Foster **excitement**

  Excitement is about students really feeling the thrill of a task, accomplishment, or experience. This may often require going the extra mile, customizing opportunities to their interest and style of learning. Creative ideas, field trips, rewards, and incentives may be involved.

Above all, parents and adults who spend time with children can set an example for critical thinking, science appreciation, and a scientific mindset. Everyone can be a STEM enthusiast and advocate, regardless of their background. Express it and expect it as much as you're comfortable doing so. If kids show interest or curiosity after looking at something, encourage them to dig deeper and help them to do so.

My son told me he chose computer science as his major because of his early exposure to the field through his extracurricular activity in robotics. Although my daughter has not yet decided on what she will pursue as a major, her science fair wins at local, state, and national levels have cemented the scientific mindset and have given her more confidence.

POINTS TO PONDER

How have you tried to support or encourage young children to appreciate science?

What strategies have worked the best in piquing their interest in STEM topics?

Curiosity[14]

Let's take a trip to curio-sity!

A place where you get to ask why? Why?? Why???

You get to wonder... and you get to learn and you even get to try...

to train the brain and stretch the mind...

to ask questions and answers find.

So, let's go there...let's ask how? let's ask where?? and let's ask why???

Let's be curious about everything...everything under the blue sky.

Wait, why is the sky blue?

Good question!

Why don't you find out...and then tell me too!

[14] Poem by Jayshree Seth. Written for her children, when they were younger.

AT HOME
With Science!

Distance living during the 2020 pandemic created a monumental shift for all of us. The rapid change created practical, technical, and emotional challenges for many, but especially parents and educators as they adapted to the necessity of distance learning. According to UNESCO, over 1.5 billion students around the world were affected by school closures in 2020.[15] In most cases, the transition was sudden. Unprecedented times called for the entire community of stakeholders to come together and be creative to keep children curious and learning.

ON HAND

Distance learning requires that we find fun and creative ways for our kids to experience interactive learning opportunities at home. As the Brookings Institution confirms, students engaged in hands-on learning are much more likely to remember what they were taught.[16] With our long history of supporting STEM education, 3M committed to doing its part to support and create quality, distance learning content for communities everywhere. We believe that, valuable as they are, you don't have to be in a classroom or lab to practice and think about science. So, 3M created an online resource of accessible science experiments called "Science at Home".[17]

Creating "Science at Home" involved a collaboration between scientists from our research teams, 3Mers from the communications team, and partners at the Bakken Museum in Minneapolis. Stretching our skillsets, scientists participated in the development, scripting, and filming of a series of short, easy-to-follow videos that led viewers through at-home science experiments with common household items. Every lesson was designed to reinforce core scientific principles. The videos were made freely available to educators, with the intent that they could use the content in their digital classrooms. Experiments were conducted with parents and kids in mind so that they could be repeated at home together safely. For subjects like science, the process of inquiry and hands-on experimentation can be key. To add to the excitement factor, we even enlisted some celebrities such as Camille Schrier, Miss America 2020.

---

[15] Henrietta Fore, "Don't let children be the hidden victims of COVID-19 pandemic," UNICEF, April 9, 2020.
[16] Bustamante and Hirsh-Pasek, "Learning about learning: Meaning matters," Brookings Institution, May 30, 2018.
[17] "3M's Commitment to Education," 3M Giving and Volunteerism, www.3M.com.

HANDS DOWN

The scientific method has long stood the test of time as being a great way to encourage kids to tinker and think about why or how things work. In fact, what we call the scientific method today comes from psychological studies of children over a hundred years ago! As Henry Cowles reveals in his discussion of the psychological "theory about theories", studying children's mental development gave psychologists a model of thinking.[18] They saw their research methods, rooted in scientific thinking, in the minds of the children they studied.

This method not only allows them to ask questions, hypothesize, and find ways to answer their questions, it can also help link what happens in the lab to the realm of ordinary life. I have shared some of my own experiences with science encouragement at home with my children. Each case was instigated by a question they raised that eventually led to a project. Whether it was *BREAD Dough D.O.E*, a simple project on understanding the science of bread-making, *Greening Under the Evergreens*, an effort to raise the pH of pine-needle laden soil under the backyard evergreen trees, or *Unleading the way*, a study on remediation of lead contaminated water inspired by the Flint water crisis, the scientific thought-process took hold. However, it was the narrative and connection to the problem that inspired and motivated them.

HANDS ON

The best part of this approach is that the scientific method of thinking is open to all regardless of comfort with science or scientific information. Children are intuitive and follow this methodology naturally. Hands-on experiences can spur curiosity in children, which is so critical to their growth and success. We need to encourage their innate curiosity and wonder. Now, more than ever, AT HOME! The steps are simple:

> **A**sk a question to articulate the problem statement
>
> **T**opical research for general understanding to plan an experiment
>
> **H**ypothesize and predict what will happen and why
>
> **O**bserve and record any data, repeat as needed
>
> **M**ake conclusions after analyzing data and interpreting the results
>
> **E**xplain conclusions and suggestions to explore the topic further

---

[18] Henry Cowles, "Child's play: The authoritative statement of scientific method derives from a surprising place - early 20th-century child psychology," Aeon, January 9, 2017.

As distance learning expands, we want to be there to support families, teachers, and students. We chart new paths together so that science and society benefit from all the many new ideas that will flow from the next generation.

POINTS TO PONDER

What are some of the challenges and outcomes of teaching science in distance learning mode?

What are some ways community stakeholders can help to address these issues?

Summer Learning Laws!
Friends and Family, Unstructured Time, and New Experiences...

"Summer learning loss" has been a topic of much discussion over the years. The term generally refers to the loss or slide in academic skills over the course of summer holidays. Studies have shown that students' achievement scores may decline over summer break by a month's worth of school-year learning.[19] Without regular practice, new skills and knowledge fade. Given the length of summer break in the United States, this can be a significant cause of concern. Many parents enroll their kids in summer programs that help to maintain skill levels, and educators recommend continued learning practice through the break. However, it is difficult to practically implement a rigorous, formal, academic schedule during summer for several reasons, including access and affordability. It is imperative to supplement learning, informally, in different ways.

SUMMER "SCHOOL"

Growing up in India, we had fairly short summer breaks, but I have countless memories of summer fun. We would look forward to trips back to the small town in our home-state to visit relatives. Whether it was spotting constellations in the clear desert nights, waking up to the sound of peacocks "meowing" in the wee hours of the morning, or hot afternoons rummaging through books and artifacts my late grandfather had collected, there was learning all around. All in all, it was an exposure to a very different environment and an educational experience of a very different kind. It is hard to determine, exactly, what role it played in our lives, but there is no question that it contributed to fundamentally shaping us and the ways we approach problems and solutions.

Times have changed in many ways. Families, specifically children, are busier. Electronic gadgets abound as peer pressure and media influence preferences and options. The competition for college placement has also further increased pressure to excel in standardized tests and extracurricular activities in order to stand-out.

SUMMER FUN

Summer learning doesn't have to be extended time or expensive trips, but just quality time with **friends and family** spent together outside of the normal routine. It is quite

---

[19] Quinn and Polikoff, "Summer learning loss: What is it, and what can we do about it?" Brookings Institution, September 14, 2017.

striking how behavior, attitudes, and expectations change with a change in scenery or roles. It appears to facilitate bonding and allow connectedness at a different level. And it is critical to developing relationships and fostering connections. Time and again it is amazing to hear from my children what they recount as a favorite memory and why.

More and more kids are engaging in more passive entertainment; playing games on phones and watching TV have replaced free playtime. Screen time doesn't count! **Unstructured time** is outside of any organized activity, it is the time that forces creative thinking, leading to self-directed activity and self-initiated efforts. This may also be the time that may allow children to find their passion. Scientists have learned that free play isn't just something children like to do, it's something they need to do.[20]

Anything that can help expand thinking and perspective facilitates learning. New places and people, food and culture, skills and training, or anything that can help to **experience the emotion of awe**. It could be trips to the zoo or museums, parks and beaches, sports and games, or fairs and festivals. Science has shown that a sense of awe can play an important role in bolstering happiness, health, and our social interactions.[21] Scientists believe it may have actually long played a role in how and why humans cooperate and collaborate.

These simple rules can help parents facilitate summer learning FUN!

Friends and Family

Unstructured time

New experiences and exposure

Summer offers a unique opportunity to engage in learning in informal ways. I have found these good rules not just for kids but us adults as well, largely rooted in the human connections that the world craves. The 2019 3M SOSI revealed that 87% would rather make five new friends in their life than 5,000 new social media followers!

So, enjoy summer... have FUN!

POINTS TO PONDER

What was your summer FUN learning like while growing up?

What other FUN activities do you think could be effective in making summer gains?

---

[20] Siobhan O'Connor, "The Secret Power of Play," Time Magazine, September 6, 2017.
[21] Emma Stone, "The Emerging Science of Awe and Its Benefits," Psychology Today, April 27, 2017.

Virtually,
A Summer of Learning...

What are some of your favorite summer memories from childhood? Many people would rank summer camps high on their list. But for millions of kids, losing summer camps due to the COVID-19 pandemic was yet another blow in 2020, as it relates to missed childhood milestones and experiences. Interactive learning opportunities and hands-on work at these kid-oriented camps gives a unique sense of community and leads to personal growth resulting in an enjoyable experience for most. Throughout the summer of 2020, after being cooped up at home for weeks, adjusting to distance-learning while separated from their friends, teachers, and classmates, kids may have needed their summer camps more than ever.

STEM-focused camps, particularly those directed at girls and underrepresented minorities, help tremendously in building a sense of community and nurturing a sense of their belonging in STEM. Fortunately, some camps were able to pivot to a remote mode on short notice while trying to maintain the learning objectives through a virtual camp. Such camps can often allow increase in enrollment, thereby increasing access, which is an additional benefit and can help with improving diversity and equity. In many cases, the current in-person model was replicated in the digital domain, real field trips became virtual expeditions, guest speakers and role models presented virtually, and demonstrations and displays switched to remote viewing. Many camps delivered supplies or "STEM kits" so that the hands-on experience could still happen, followed by online exhibitions at the end of the week where students could showcase their work.

CAMP CONSTERNATION

It is often said that relationships are the foundation of learning; when students feel connected to their peers and teachers, they're more likely to thrive.[22] And it is indeed tough to create that sense of connectedness without physically coming together in a group setting. Additionally, the many benefits of face-to-face interaction, including more spontaneous conversations that can spark new ideas or create new friendships are perhaps hard to create in a virtual mode, especially with pre-teen girls. I recently got the opportunity to have a "virtual lunch" with the young participants of an all-girls STEM camp. During the planning sessions, I was alerted to the fact that

---

[22]Dennis Pierce, "Five ways to build a community of learners online," eSchool News, June 11, 2020.

while I speak to them, many will not have their video-mode on! In "The STEAM Engine That Could!", I discuss the problem of female underrepresentation in STEM and ways to engage more girls through exposure. However, 2020 posed a particularly tough challenge, as most kids suddenly transitioned to distance-learning.

For my virtual lunch, I had to adapt and rely largely on storytelling. And, with no visual cues to their reactions to what I was saying or showing, I resorted to asking a lot of questions in attempts to engage them. I relied on past interactions with kids and my experiences with my own daughter. Instead of focusing the conversation on my educational background, current role, and projects, I talked about why I like being a scientist: solving problems creatively, innovating and inventing to help people, and improving lives with sustainable innovation. I also talked about the fun-factor: traveling the world, working with people from around the globe, and being on TV!

I kept asking questions, and finally, their questions started coming in. I was able to use their questions as an opportunity to weave in my educational background, current role, and projects that they could relate to, like my work on diaper fasteners for wiggly babies.

It became apparent that facilitating pivotal conversations remotely can tap into a student's sense of curiosity and wonder, though it is much easier to ask the probing questions in a face-to-face setting. Initiating these conversations is something parents can engage in as well to extend learning. I have previously talked about the importance of encouraging kids to look into something rather than looking at it.

(RE)BOOT CAMP

Interestingly all the challenges of a sudden transition to virtual mode impacted many aspects of work as well. The same challenges were apparent as I connected with new employees on-boarding during the pandemic. I also spoke to 3M interns whose internship was rendered virtual during uncertain times. Some companies scrapped their intern programs altogether, but 3M got creative and provided access and opportunity to contribute while remote. A critical part of the intern experience is, of course, being on campus and interacting with the many 3Mers in casual and informal settings. Although that could not happen for many, the inevitable tradeoffs led to certain benefits in 2020. For example, the interns got to hear from senior leaders who may have otherwise been on the road.

Nonetheless, for any virtual program adapted from a physical one, there needs to be a concerted effort to foster a sense of community given that everyday casual interactions were limited in the virtual mode. There is perhaps a lot to be learned from the experiences, and especially grievances, of those who had been working remotely even prior to the pandemic. Most experts agree that a critical element to remote work is a focus on meaningful connections to prevent a feeling of isolation. It is critical to gauge engagement with regular check-ins while continuing conscious communications.

Be it summer camps, interns, new employees, or for that matter, veteran employees, a transition from physical to virtual models requires time to adjust. We also need techniques to connect participants at the human level, especially if they do not have the benefit of knowing each other. This calls for well-designed tools and incentives for social engagement, as well as well-trained practitioners who can foster a sense of connectedness, the kind that feels authentic and not contrived. It calls for learning and stretching outside of our own comfort zone for most of us. It is as if we are all in camps, which calls for patience with ourselves, those we interact with, and the technology that helps facilitate it all.

Communications for connectedness

Adaptation with adoption

Mentoring while monitoring

Patience and persistence

Success in access

If we can learn and master these elements, we will all be happy campers!

POINTS TO PONDER

What are some of the techniques that have worked well when working remotely as an online participant?

What do you enjoy most about your office? Is there a way to recreate the element(s) in a virtual world?

"Management that is destructively critical when mistakes are made kills initiative. And it's essential that we have many people with initiative if we are to continue to grow."

— William L. McKnight, 3M President (1929-1949)
and Chairman of the Board (1949-1966)

Raising Innovation:
The Six Most Common ERRORS!

Over the last few years, I have given several keynotes at various forums around the world on the topic of innovation. There is tremendous interest in the "secret sauce." Fostering creativity and innovation in a corporate setting is certainly not child's play, but can be made easier if a few fundamentally essential elements are addressed. Six elements, to be precise. At least, that has been my experience at work and at home.

When my kids were little, I told them, "Don't buy me gifts, make them with your own hands instead." It started out with the "Haqqy Birthbay!" scrawled by their tiny hands to sign projects done at daycare. But slowly, I could see them applying themselves to take what they had learned and actually create new artwork, specifically for gift-giving. With at least four opportunities per year to give mommy a gift, I also noticed a distinct change in their thought process as they learned new skills. They were always evaluating the potential of what they had learned to being able to use it to make a gift.

Then the requests started: special markers, origami paper, sewing kits, and knitting needles... and we happily obliged. "Mommy is super-excited to see what she will get for Valentine's day!" The requests, and the gifts, got more and more creative. I encouraged our son to participate in the annual coloring contest hosted every year by our leading newspaper. He replied, "But we are vegetarians, we don't even eat turkey!" It took some convincing, and a few years, but "Lentil Turkey" won him a prize. A picture of his turkey, adorned with colorful lentils, was published in the local paper. The gift card was used to buy more origami paper.

When he perfected a few more origami objects, I suggested he make and sell them at his Saturday School for Indian Languages and Culture to raise money for tsunami victims in Japan. The "Origami for Tsunami" fundraising was successful, and he was proud to send in the check to Red Cross for money collected from selling peace cranes. The local paper did an article on his endeavor. He was excited to get Lego NXT as a reward from us for the good deed. It fortified his love for robotics and programming, and eventually, his decision to pursue computer science as a major in college. His college application material did mention the children's book that his mom wrote, and he illustrated, when he was 10!

CREATIVE COMMONS

Our daughter, who is four years younger, was on-boarded into the family
tradition, socialized with this concept of making gifts for mommy. Blessed with a very
different temperament, she just wanted to know what she could do to get in the
newspaper like bhaiyya (older brother). Perhaps recognizing her lack of patience for
intricate art projects, she started relying more on her ability to write. The poems
got more meaningful and with less predictable rhyming patterns as time went on.
Multi-media presentations were put together as gifts.

When we watched Malala's speech at the U.N. Youth Assembly, I could see it
pique my daughter's interest. "One child, one teacher, one pen, and one book can
change the world."[23] I encouraged her to research Malala's story and put together a
presentation for her social studies class. That led to the "Minnesota for Malala"
book-drive. She loved being in the newspaper. It was a reward in itself that motivated
her to do more. And then there was the, "Mommy doesn't want cake, maybe we can
make sweeter whole-wheat bread for her birthday!" The what-happens-when-you-
double-the-sugar-in-our-homemade-bread-recipe led to another series of experiments.
Working with my husband, she investigated the outcomes of making bread with twice
the amount of key ingredients, which we willingly ate. Community and science
projects continued through middle school, with accolades at local, state, and national
level, and sustained through high school. We helped her file her first patent.

ROUNDING ERRORS

In my experience, although the topic is a little more complex and multifaceted, not
much is different for fostering creativity and innovation within the corporate context.
Unless one is intrinsically highly motivated, the rest of us deliver better when there is
a general **expectation** of a certain behavior. This expectation can change the way we
think and operate. In addition, with **resources** and encouragement to take **risk**, we
feel the freedom to be more creative, in our own way. If there is ample **opportunity**
for collaboration and support to champion, lead, and implement our ideas, we are
inspired to deliver commercial results. The associated **reward** and recognition for
successful value creation further inspire us to innovate. Above all, the continued
socialization of the concept of being innovative and its place in a company's culture,
and link to rewards and recognition, helps sustain it. It's about the stories that are
communicated and the narrative that lives on.

Many companies know this. I am fortunate to be working at one with a
long-standing culture that encourages employee initiative and innovation while
providing enabling resources, an environment of creativity and cooperation, and a

---

[23]Malala Yousafzai, 2013 United Nations Youth Assembly

growth mindset that drives us to take ideas to inventions and product innovations to delight our customers.

These are the key elements to be considered for fostering and preserving a successful culture of innovation and a lack of system level approach to any of them would be a mistake!

Expectation

Resources

Risk-taking

Opportunity

Reward

Socialization

Innovation is often reduced to a buzzword. Inculcating, maintaining, and sustaining a true culture of innovation...takes just that, innovation.

POINTS TO PONDER

What have you seen work well in developing and promoting a mindset or culture of innovation?

What, in your experience, are elements that can deter innovation within an organization?

*"I am always interested in learning something new.
I like to learn. That's an art and a science."*

— Katherine Johnson, NASA Mathematician and Physicist

The STEAM Engine That Could!
Overcoming the Problem
of Female Underrepresentation

Do you remember the first time you saw a "scientist"? Was it in a movie or a comic strip? Or did you conjure up the image from a book you read? Were they all men? It wouldn't surprise me if they were, it would certainly be consistent with media portrayal of scientists over the years. Thankfully, the image has improved, moving away from mad or evil scientist stereotypes that could negatively impact how girls, like my daughter, identify with STEM. The media representation of females and minorities in scientific fields has also increased due to better mentorship efforts and cultural movements such as International Women's Day (March 8).

United Nations (U.N.) Secretary-General Antonio Guterres marked the 2019 International Day of Women and Girls in Science with the following words: "Let's ensure that every girl, everywhere, has the opportunity to realize her dreams, grow into her power and contribute to a sustainable future for all." He went on to stay that gender stereotypes, a lack of visible role models, and unsupportive or even hostile policies and environments can keep women and girls from pursuing these careers. His call to action was for "concerted, concrete efforts" to overcome these obstacles.

The world must not only tackle misconceptions about girls' abilities, but it must also promote access to learning opportunities for women and girls. U.N. officials put it succinctly: the future will be marked by scientific and technological progress which, "will be the greatest when it draws on the full talent, creativity and ideas of women and girls in science."[24]

S.T.E.A.M. CLEANING

I believed things would be different for my daughter. I envisioned that her connection to science would be more about interest and aptitude, and perhaps having a role model right at home. So, imagine my surprise when she showed reluctance toward attending an after-school science activity, saying, "I don't want to be a scientist. I am not a nerd. I want to help people!" It was clear to my husband and I, two engineers with Ph.D.s, that we had failed to *market* to our daughter what

---

[24] U.N. News, "Ahead of International Day of Women and Girls in Science, UN calls for smashing stereotypes," February 9, 2018.

science is *and* what scientists do! We certainly hadn't mastered the *art of communi-cating science* to a young impressionable mind, influenced by media stereotypes and pop-culture portrayals. We also didn't emphasize the connection of how science solves problems and benefits others, something important to our daughter and countless young girls. Could this be the key to attracting young girls to STEM?

We began the journey of explaining *why* the science was important instead of simply sharing the *what*. In our case, as an example, this meant explaining how mommy's new invention helps diapers stay put on wiggly babies, and how daddy's new window film helps make rooms more comfortable for the occupants. These stories gave our daughter the much-needed context to pique her curiosity. From there, we nurtured this curiosity and helped her develop creativity, problem-solving, and critical thinking skills with project-based learning. Learning doesn't only happen in the classroom or the workplace.

Once her passion for a subject was established, she was excited to do the work and felt pride in explaining her experiments and discoveries. We even encouraged her to participate in local science fairs. I've mentioned that one of my daughter's favorite projects was *Bread Dough D.O.E.*, a simple project about the science of bread-making by changing ratios of key ingredients. We have seen the scientific thought process take hold, but each time it is the narrative and connection to the problem that inspires and motivates her. It is the injection of the A (art) in STEM that makes her go full STEAM ahead! Whether or not she chooses to pursue a career in STE(A)M, I think we have *cleaned* up her misconceptions and bolstered her appreciation for everyday science. We have succeeded in making science more interesting for her.

LETTING OFF SOME S.T.E.A.M.

Beyond personal anecdotes, the data tell us that there is work to be done. In the 2018 3M SOSI, we learned that 25% of women and 22% of men say they find science boring, globally. The results also showed that women trail men in positive sentiment for science across a number of survey questions and responses. So, how do we get more people, particularly girls, interested in science?

Persisting biases and gender stereotypes, perhaps in combination with some evolutionary hardwiring or social conditioning, can drive girls and women away from science-related fields. A study published in 2017 in *Science* shows that by age six, girls are already less likely than boys to describe their own gender as "brilliant", and are likely to turn down the opportunity to participate in activities said to be for "very, very smart" children.[25] But, at age five, just one year earlier, there was no differentiation

---

[25] Bian, Leslie, and Cimpian, 2017. "Gender stereotypes about intellectual ability emerge early and influence children's interests," Science.

between boys and girls in expectations of "really, really smart". Parents, teachers, society, workplace culture, and women all have a role to play in addressing the issue.

As depicted in the film *Hidden Figures*, the early days of electronic computing, the work was largely done by women! Once computers became indispensable and associated with great power and influence, female programmers lost out in **Technology** despite having all the requisite skills. A.I. recruiting processes continue the industry's legacy of bias because these jobs are located in already male-dominated fields filled with men's resumes.[26] Now, it's time for men to stand up as allies and vocal advocates, not just at work but also at home. Girls need to see more young women in tech roles and young women need to see more role models succeeding in tech. They need to believe that STEM fields include environments that will allow them to have fulfilling careers and lives.

A study conducted by Microsoft found that 72% of the girls polled said it was important for them to have jobs that directly helped the world, but only 37% thought of STEM careers as being creative or making the world better.[27] The solution is right there for us, the very narrative around **Engineering** needs to be re-engineered! I have seen first-hand the impact of girls' strong desire to change the world. My daughter was interested in pursuing science projects when she realized they would solve real-world problems and help others. The context was way more important to her than the concept or content. We need to "help girls connect the dots between changing the world and STEM."[28]

Scientists have long recognized that science and the **Art** of storytelling are inextricably intertwined, and Rachel Hutter, Senior Vice President, The Walt Disney Company, says it well when she asserts that "the intersection of engineering and the arts is innovation." Unfortunately, in a standardized testing driven environment there is often no room left for creativity. Students are introduced to core scientific concepts largely through textbooks and lectures that can be perceived rather uninspiring. Interactive experiences, exposure to STEM careers, and visibility of role-models will go a long way in inspiring more girls. If STEM subjects were explained through the lens of story, it is believed that many more girls, who consistently score higher than boys in verbal proficiency, might be more interested. "It sure beats a pink microscope!"[29]

The 2018 Future of Jobs Report by the World Economic Forum, covering 20 countries, concluded that millions of jobs could be lost to disruptive labor market

[26] Marie Hicks, "Why tech's gender problem is nothing new," The Guardian, October 12, 2018.
[27] Clare McGrane, "Misconceptions and stereotypes may discourage girls from studying STEM, study finds," GeekWire, March 13, 2018.
[28] Talia Milgrom-Elcott, "Girls, If You Want To Change The World", Try STEM," Forbes, September 11, 2018.
[29] Anna Kuchment, "To Attract More Girls to STEM, Bring More Storytelling to Science," Scientific American, April 16, 2013.

changes with an overwhelming majority of future jobs requiring STEM-based skills.[30]
The **Math** is simple, we cannot afford to miss out on the contributions of 50% of the
world's population! We need that diversity of thought, especially when there are many
critical problems waiting to be solved creatively. We need numbers, governance,
and policy and diversity and inclusion and goals and metrics...

FULL S.T.E.A.M. AHEAD

There is a lot of momentum around gender equality in STEM. It is apparent what
needs to happen to increase the representation of women, and many initiatives are
driving change.

> **S**hattering of stereotypes
>
> **T**elling the whole(some) story
>
> **E**xposure and environment
>
> **A**llies and advocates
>
> **M**etrics and measures

Diversity of thought, and ideas, is going to be the lifeblood for tackling societal
challenges. No one has a monopoly on creative ideas and innovation. It is imperative
that we have strong representation from women and minorities to unlock the secrets
of building a sustainable future for all of us. Of course, I didn't know this when I
enrolled in engineering. As I mentioned, I grew up in a University town in India
with a premier engineering institute, surrounded by male scientists and engineers.
Local parents often *pushed* their daughters into the field of engineering so they
would go to the local college and stay close to home.

As U.N. Secretary-General Guterres said, "We need to encourage and support
girls and women achieve their full potential as scientific researchers and innovators.
Women and girls need this, and the world needs this, if we are to achieve our
ambitions for sustainable development on a healthy planet."

POINTS TO PONDER

What experiences or exposure motivated you to pursue a STEM education?

What role did role models play in your educational journey or your career path?

---

[30] World Economic Forum, "The Future of Jobs Report 2018," September 17, 2018.

Raising Influence in Science and Engineering:
RISE and Shine!

Beyoncé got it right! (My son gets the credit for introducing me to the lyrics in "Bigger".) The idea of being part of something bigger than yourself really resonated with my audience of underrepresented minorities (URM) in STEM. Women, Black, and Latinx students were selected to attend the inaugural, 2020 3M R.I.S.E. Event, Raising Influence in Science and Engineering. The program was created to introduce emerging female and underrepresented science and engineering graduate talent to the wide range of rewarding careers in research and development. The three-day program, which pivoted to a virtual format due to the pandemic, gave these bright minds the opportunity to hear about technology, products, and platforms, and to interact with scientists about their research and career experiences. Top executives also attended and talked about our vision, the culture, and their commitment to building a diverse workforce. Diversity, inclusion, and equity have long been values at 3M.

SHINE A LIGHT

I was curious to know what was on the mind of this emerging, diverse talent pool and requested questions be sent ahead of time so I could address them in my keynote presentation. It was impressive to see how many participants took the time to send detailed questions about various aspects of corporate life and my career journey, as well as seeking advice on what constitutes a successful career from my perspective. It was most interesting to see an overwhelming majority ask what made me stay for 27 years, which included questions about 3M culture, commitment to diversity, and our work on STEM advocacy and equity.

Research indeed shows that members of groups underrepresented in STEM fields (i.e. women, racial and ethnic minorities, and first generation college students) tend to value communal goals to a greater extent than members of groups that are better represented.[31] Research also shows that, among STEM students, women and URM are disproportionately interested in using their degrees to make the world more equitable and fair. When students perceive the availability of communal opportunities, they experience heightened belonging. By the same token, a disconnect or

---

[31] Boucher et al., 2017. "Can I work with and Help Others in This Field? How Communal Goals Influence Interest and Participation in STEM Fields," Frontiers in Psychology.

incongruity with communal goals can negatively influence underrepresented racial and ethnic minority students' overall success in school, research, and in their careers.[32] It is essential that we not only provide communal opportunities for the greater good of society, but precisely because those are the opportunities that will allow us to attract and retain the very diversity we know we need to continue to thrive.

RISING TIDE

I have previously talked about the desire to improve lives and make the world a better place when I was growing up. I didn't quite see the contextual connection with STEM careers as a student, but due to strong parental guidance I pursued an engineering degree anyway and made shifts when I sensed communal goal incongruity, or the lack of strong engagement in a topic due to the perceived absence of connection to communal goals.[33] A strong culture of collaboration at 3M, allowed me to succeed, inspired by our vision for improving lives and a commitment to sustainability. I candidly shared with the R.I.S.E. participants, that success, as I defined it for myself, is a career that affords both communal and agentic opportunities. I know this was important to share because research shows that given the heightened sensitivity, or cognitive predisposition of URMs and women to strongly endorse communal goals, they are more sensitive to cues that signal the presence or absence of communal opportunities.

Women and URMs are also more likely to seek and notice opportunities that involve helping, collaborating, and developing relationships with people. They typically focus less on agency, which involves a drive for one's self in terms of one's own achievement, status, and independence. I wanted to combat any stereotypical beliefs regarding who enters, persists, and excels in corporate STEM careers. Collaboration and the storied "15% Culture" at 3M empowers us to work with others and help them. I also mentioned my roles over the years in Technical Forum, Technical Council, CEO Inclusion Council, Employee Resource Networks, and Community Service Project in Ghana, which are all examples of how communal experiences are embedded into the organizational structure, systems and culture at 3M. And that is why I did not perceive what is referred to as communal goal incongruity. Instead, I stayed.

RISE TOGETHER

I also took the opportunity to share my view on why a culture of empowerment works, the role of management, and how I viewed my own job and expectations of self. I explore each of these topics in later articles. I talked about collaborating with

[32] Gray et al., 2020. "Engaging Black and Latinx students through communal learning opportunities: A relevance intervention for middle schoolers in STEM elective classrooms," Contemporary Educational Psychology.
[33] Diekman and Steinberg, 2013. "Navigating Social Roles in Pursuit of Important Goals: A Communal Goal Congruity Account of STEM Pursuits," Social and Personality Psychology Compass.

others, bringing in not just my functional knowledge but my own unique strengths and perspective given my intersectionality in various vectors of diversity. I gave examples of taking initiative to continuously inform, expand my sphere of influence, and inspire from my own rung of the ladder.

I also talked about the struggles with confidence in my journey of authenticity, especially when I was called upon to be the company's first-ever Chief Science Advocate. For me achieving success in new roles and groundbreaking initiatives, in large part, has been due to the ability to establish relationships. This was accomplished, not by focusing on the differences, but by authentically bonding around the abundance of similarities and commonalities we share at a very human level. I've learned that one cannot assume that people will not be willing to learn and change simply because they do not perceive a given change to work to their benefit. Hearts and minds can be changed.

I try to carry the same message in our science advocacy work, given the results of 3M SOSI. It has indeed been a journey of finding my voice and using it, and now, amplifying it with the platform I have been given. I also shared my perspective on the crises in 2020 as well as my views on the path forward, which I explore in the last section of this book. No doubt I have encountered *failures* along the way, but I passed along the importance of keeping perspective. Though I question if things can be called a failure if something was truly learned!

If I was writing a song about my STEM journey, the lyrics would be about:

> **R**esponsibility – raising influence
>
> Initiative – take it!
>
> Similarity, commonality – humanity
>
> Expectations – of self and others

In addition to organizational culture and practices, one's own personal attributes, knowledge, aptitude, and overall attitude play a strong role in career success. RISE! Hold your head high and shine with positive energy.

POINTS TO PONDER

*What challenges have you, or someone you know,
overcome as an URM in STEM fields?*

*What additional advice would you give to women
and other URM looking to pursue a career in STEM?*

#GenerationEquality[34]

Imagine a world where all the people
...have rights and opportunities that are equal.
A world where there is equal joy... when a baby girl...
or a boy...is born.
In a world, where gender equality is the norm.
Women feel safe. Women have an equal say.
And for the work they do... women, they get equal pay.
Where men share... in the care.
And women dare...to dream of studying anything...
of working... anywhere.
Women's rights for an equal future...nothing wrong
with this picture...
...there are no glass ceilings, there are seats at the table,
...there is equity in the classroom, in the boardroom
and on that factory floor.
And in this world, opportunity comes knocking,
equally, at every door.
Our strength is diversity, the goal equality
...making gender equity, a lived reality.
This world ...it's for you, it's for me, it's for every person!
No matter your race, your gender, your religion.
No matter where you live, no matter who you love,
...no matter your age or your affiliation.
I, imagine a world where all the people
...have rights and opportunities that are equal.
I am...
I am...
I am...
Generation Equality

---

[34]Written by Jayshree Seth for International Women's Day, 2020

SECTION 3

Leadership
*On the Need for Leading from
Our Own Rung of the Ladder*

"I believe that the capacity that any organisation needs is for leadership to appear anywhere it is needed, when it is needed."

— Margaret J. Wheatley, Leadership and the New Science

The Five Views of Leadership:
What's in Your Scope?

Do you ever think about the role of luck in your career? Perhaps you've experienced a chance meeting that resulted in a career opportunity? Was there an unexpected project shift that turned out well for you? Did you get the *right* leader at just the *right* time?

Recent research suggests that just being prompted to recognize luck can encourage generosity.[35] When we acknowledge the importance of luck, we are much more likely to share some of our own good fortune for the common good. This acceptance of luck, and a feeling of gratitude, is very important for good leaders in top positions. How you view top leadership qualities can help you balance technical and empathetic skills.

A SPECTRUM OF VIEWS

Metaphorical thinking is a powerful tool often used to visualize leadership concepts. For instance, microscopes and telescopes can be good metaphors for short-term *and* long-term views, respectively. Both of these "scopes" can provide a view that is not visible to the naked eye. Great leaders possess the ability to view both, and they have a keen understanding of when to use which one. Leaders also realize that the detailed microscopic view of the short-term has to be consistent to realize the telescope's vision.

What happens when people have grandiose telescope vision but do not understand the necessary details to turn the vision into reality? The 2018 3M SOSI revealed that people have tremendous expectations of what science will achieve in the near future: flying cars, living on Mars, teleportation, undersea living and more. But in the same survey, 38% said if science didn't exist, their everyday lives wouldn't be any different! This telescopic view aligns with the idea that significantly more people believe science is very important to society in general (63%) than it is to their daily, microscopic lives.

With the rate of disruption in virtually every industry, the periscope view becomes an important metaphor as well. A periscope is designed to look over and around obstacles that may be obstructing one's view. For 3M and other companies, it's important to continually look outside our immediate surroundings to identify major trends and threats in the market, specifically how they will impact the products, platforms, and

---

[35]Robert H. Frank, "Why Luck Matters More Thank You Might Think," The Atlantic, May 2016.

business models. A keen view through a periscope is critical because it can call for an adjustment of the telescopic and microscopic views to which we're accustomed.

DISCOVERING WHAT YOU CAN'T SEE

Think about your senses for a moment. How can you hear things you might not be able to see? With another tool: a stethoscope. Good leaders need to listen to their heart and intuition to engage their teams in ways that might not be tangible. This is very important, especially since research indicates disengaged employees lead to lost productivity.[36] Much has been written about leading with heart, and inspiring constituencies by capturing their hearts. [37]

Finally, there is the horoscope, the good or bad luck that we will encounter because it was part of our fate. Many times, though we can do our best and hope for the best, the rest we may not be able to control. It doesn't mean that we resort to inaction because it's not up to us; it means we do the right thing without being attached to the fruits of the labor. People may not like to acknowledge the role of luck in their work, as it undermines this feeling of being in control.

PUTTING IT INTO PRACTICE

- The **telescope:** *Look far ahead...*

  Ask yourself where you are going and see what the big picture is for the team.

- The **microscope:** *Look deep down...*

  Think about what you are doing, delving deeply to see the detailed view, the critical functioning, and the execution in the short term.

- The **periscope:** *Look out! Look over, back, & around...*

  See what is not in direct line of sight. Anticipate change and proactively identify opportunities.

- The **stethoscope:** *Look within...*

  See what cannot be seen but only felt. Listen to the heart, your own and others, to inform and inspire.

- The **horoscope:** *Look above...*

  See and acknowledge what you can't control. Be grateful for the role of luck and chance. Humility makes for authentic leaders.

---

[36]Govindarajan and Srinivas, "The Innovation Mindset in Action: 3M Corporation," Harvard Business Review, August 6, 2013.
[37]Suzanne Degges-White, "Leading from the Heart," Psychology Today, February 5, 2015.

Good leaders strive to use all of these views to enjoy the **kaleidoscope** of true leadership. I, for one, have really learnt to value the *horoscope*. Although intrinsically motivated and conscientious, I certainly can't take complete credit for my career. It's natural to want to take credit for success, for having worked hard and earned it, but it feels more authentic to appreciate the role of luck along the journey. Acknowledging luck is a humbling experience, and it fills you with gratitude and appreciation for the opportunities you have been afforded. *My mantra: Remember, it's not just you, its your kismet and your karma that come along on the journey too.*

POINTS TO PONDER

*How are you actively integrating
all the "scopes" in your view?*

*What challenges do you see as you balance
the kaleidoscope of your leadership?*

Of Leaders and Ladders:
Can You Lead Without Being "The Boss"?

Do you remember what you wanted to be when you grew up? Was it a teacher, a physician, or a small business owner? After all, those are some of the most visible people in our early lives. Each of these professions have something important in common: you don't need to rise to the topmost rank to become leaders. For instance, a teacher's positive impact can be felt in the classroom and beyond whether or not they have aspirations of becoming a principal or superintendent. This same logic can exist in other careers, too.

We typically have narrow views of leadership until we see it firsthand. When my daughter was in elementary school, she declared that she had figured out what she wanted to be when she grew up. We were all ears. "I want to be the boss." Her reasoning? Simple: "I want to tell others what to do!"

WHO'S THE BOSS?

It isn't just kids who have a very naïve notion of what it means to be a boss. As a new entrant into the corporate world, straight out of graduate school, armed with a Ph.D., and never having worked before, I was pretty much in the same boat. When I started my career at 3M, I was exposed to many different kinds of colleagues in R&D. Among them, I observed three distinct roles, including people in technical management roles that didn't appear to fit my definition of a "leader", those who I perceived as key leaders but didn't have a management title, and scientists and engineers who loved being in the lab setting and would never consider management track roles.

But over the years there was more clarity around what constituted the complex kaleidoscope of true leadership and its relationship with organizational hierarchy. I interacted with managers who were not really viewed as leaders and people I perceived as leaders who were not even in management. I worked with many scientists and engineers who would never ever consider, even in their dreams, a supervisory role on the corporate ladder towards executive leadership. But among them were also the people who could inspire towards action and influence others without authority. I soon realized that many of these colleagues were "natural born leaders". They found ways to grow in their career, coaching, mentoring, and influencing others, while never really missing out on the action in the lab. They could clearly articulate a vision and pull teams together to steer work towards a goal.

Before long, I was at a crossroads in my own career. I had just completed an assignment on improving work processes and coaching product development teams as a Design for Six Sigma Black Belt, when I was presented with the opportunity to move into people management. I would be exposed to a new way of thinking and change my career path to be on a management track. I had to do some soul-searching. I was unsure how my strengths and weaknesses would play out in a management role, especially given my desire to stay authentic to my true self. I also had to take stock of my personal life. My husband and I wanted to be present parents, and I wasn't sure about the flexibility of management roles at the time. Would I have to give up things that were important to me, like preparing home-cooked meals together or taking time to expose our kids to elements of Indian culture?

After agonizing for weeks, my then-boss gave me a simple piece of advice that brought instant clarity. She said, "Make the best decision *for you, for now.*"

I AM THE BOSS!

I decided to stay at the bench instead of pursuing the management leadership track. Looking back, I had realized, deep down, that the notion of "thought leadership" at work was very important to me. Empowered by our culture of innovation, I wanted to take initiative, champion new ideas, and hopefully have impact. I knew I could do it without formal authority and avail myself with the "dual career ladder" at 3M.

Today, I am just as passionate to learn, imagine, and create as I was when I first started my career decades years ago. My primary work still comes to life in a lab setting; I feel especially connected to the place where my love for science and research was born alongside the technology and products we've helped create. I am confident that this is the right decision for me, for now. If circumstances change, I can still decide to pursue an alternate path. Everyone's career journey is unique based on what they value in their professional and personal lives.

I hope my daughter gets to become "the boss", but above all, I hope she can be a good leader. I hope she learns that leadership isn't just about having a title! Leadership is more about vision and influence than it is about "telling people what to do". Ultimately, the "I"s have it, it's up to *you!*

Initiative • Inform • Influence • Inspire • Impact

You don't need to climb the corporate ladder to the top-most ranks to become a leader. We can all try to take initiative, inform, influence, and inspire to have impact right from our own rung.

POINTS TO PONDER

How did you make major career path decisions?

What do you do to lead from your rung?

Move Over SMART Goals,
I'm SUPER Smart...!

From time-to-time, I wonder if most big companies will eventually adopt a different model of goal setting and associated performance management. In our roles today, we manage unprecedented levels of complexity, grapple with uncertainty, maneuver through ambiguity, and display organizational ambidexterity, often with a backdrop of global diversity and budgetary austerity. I think that deserves a new model!

Our jobs have evolved from, or need to evolve from, managing outcomes using the time-honored SMART goals (Specific, Measurable, Achievable, Relevant, Time-bound). Our goals relate to, or need to relate to, accomplishing not only what is deemed strategically important in the short term for our strategic vision, but also what may be potentially significant to its success in the mid to long term. We need to attend to critically urgent matters that may arise much later than the formal goal setting process can accommodate at the beginning of the year. We need to formalize adaptation.

During the course of the year, we must identify and follow through on reasonably prudent things that can impact our business. It is imperative we remain flexible and potentially take on added responsibility based on our assessment of emerging trends. Through all of this, in a company like mine, we also need to continually respect the opportunity we have and remain active in "giving-back", such as mentoring and furthering the goals of our larger organizations with participation in corporate initiatives and committees.

STREET SMART

SMART goals just seem too simplistic now. They certainly don't capture the holistic essence of most jobs, and they seem to address very limited dimensions of what we do, or should do, to drive growth for organizations. They may still be applicable to a subset of what we do, but it would be a very limited subset for mid- to senior-level, corporate roles. Above all, SMART goals can fall short in sparking the imagination or inspiring to aspire for greater things for ourselves and our organizations.

Maybe, it is time to say, "***I'm SUPER*** smart!" I will do things that are:

Strategically	**Im**portant
Potentially	**S**ignificant
Critically	**U**rgent
Reasonably	**P**rudent
Flexibility for	**E**mergent
Continually	**R**everent

Maybe, it is time to put more soul into our goals!

POINTS TO PONDER

*What do you think are some limitations
of traditional SMART goals?*

*What elements of your role are not adequately
incorporated into your appraisal?*

Three Simple Ways Managers Can Sweeten Relationships:
And It's Not About Candy Coating!

Fifty percent of employees quit their jobs citing dissatisfaction with their managers![38]

As I reflect upon my own career, I can now clearly see what my managers did that helped to foster an environment of trust and convey that they really wanted to help me succeed. Employee engagement and effectiveness is highly correlated with a strong manager-employee relationship, built on mutual trust. Oftentimes, it is not the pay or the perks or the privileges that are critical to retaining high-performing employees, but a positive working relationship with their immediate management. So, apart from the functional management of roles, responsibilities, and results, how did my managers foster a trusting relationship?

I can think of three main elements related to their responses to the following situations.

- **Can-do!**

  The space that exists when you're motivated and passionate about something, willing to take initiative and pursue an idea independently.

- **Can-I-do?**

  The occasions when you are more tentative about an assignment or opportunity that has come your way.

- **Candid...**

  The moments when it is important for managers to be honest in their feedback.

BOX OF CHOCOLATES

When I was in a *can-do mode*, my managers didn't try to talk me out of it. By the same token, they didn't try to make it all about them. Instead, they placed trust in my planning, championing, and decision-making capabilities. They asked how they could be of assistance as I pursued my ideas further. There was a recognition that individual initiative is often where it all starts, and it certainly helped that I worked in a company that believes strongly in the power of employee initiative. It is well-accepted that taking

---

[38] Harter and Adkins, "Employees Want a Lot More From Their Managers," Gallup, April 8, 2015.

initiative should be encouraged because it not only builds self-confidence and enriches experience-set for effectiveness, but it builds engagement and can lead to tremendous growth for the company.

When I was in *can-I-do mode*, my managers listened to me, acknowledged my feelings and opinions, and helped me work through the feelings or thoughts that were holding me back. The so called "confidence gap" between men and women has now been well documented, and I speak to it in depth in the next section. Compared to many men, women often don't consider themselves ready for challenging roles because they often underestimate their own competence. I am thankful my managers helped me see the way by reassuring me and providing more context that connected me to a broader purpose with the new role or responsibility. Again, company culture played a critical role in this, and I benefited from managers who value diversity and placed trust in my capabilities.

When I had *candid* feedback coming my way, my managers coached me on how to manage my weaknesses and continue to build upon my strengths. Though their feedback wasn't sugar-coated, it was handled in a positive way that was empowering. The backdrop of their intentions was always about making me more effective in my endeavors. This allowed me to take the feedback to heart, try to adjust my style, and approach change in an authentic fashion. Clearly, no one's perfect, but everyone ought to continually work towards being as effective as they can be to achieve desired results. Oftentimes, it involves being coached to tweak one's personal style, which my managers did.

I believe all leaders, managers, supervisors can try these three simple ways of building trust with your employees.

- **Cultivate** *"Can-do!"*

  Once you see it, *get out* of the way.
  Tip: Start the conversation with, *"How can I help...?"*

- **Counsel the** *"Can-I-do?"*

  Gently help them see the way.
  Tip: Consider phrases like, *"Maybe I can help with that..."*

- **Coach,** *candidly.*

  Show the way... *and the why.*
  Tip: Think of it as, *"I need you to help me help you..."*

Allow people to lead, innovate and ultimately contribute effectively towards achieving the company's growth objectives. Using these simple strategies should help managers hit the sweet spot!

POINTS TO PONDER

How have managers, mentors, or advisers cultivated, counseled, or coached you effectively?

How do you effectively cultivate, counsel, and coach others to their strengths and weaknesses?

The One-Word Secret to Giving
Good TALKS...!

I often recommend to many mentees, especially in the technical community, to consider committing to improving communication and public speaking skills. This is something we can all improve to maximize our impact and is a necessary element of effective leadership. There are an overwhelming number of TED Talks on how to give better talks. However, if we break it down to the essentials, it is fairly simple: the word TALKS says it all!

Topic

Audience

Layout

Key points

Story

We can consciously work on these aspects as we prepare for our talks. A little bit of upfront work can go a long way toward delivering an effective presentation. Is it the right **topic** for the event? Is enough time allotted? Am I the right speaker, and what particular aspect of the topic is of interest? Accordingly, what should be the abstract for the presentation, and how can I engage folks with a meaningful title for it?

Which brings us to the ever-important **audience**. Who is likely to be there? How much background will be needed? What would they want to know? What would I want to know if I was in the audience? Is it an audience of stakeholders? Technical peers? Marketing, sales, and business folks? Upper management? Each of these groups will require special preparation to deliver an effective message.

TALKING POINTS

For setting up the **layout** of presentations, I use what I call the ABCDEFG technique; another reminder to cover all aspects.

- **A**genda/Abstract/Outline
  Seek permission (and commitment) right at the beginning

- **B**ackground/Affiliation
  Situate the audience (set expectations)

- **C**ontext/Relevance
  Communicate why this is important to talk about (provide the backdrop)

- **D**ata/Conclusions
  "Tell them what you are going to tell them, and tell them what you just told them"

- **E**numerate Issues/Challenges
  And tie the issues to the next steps/timeline/needs

- **F**inal Summary
  Recap the "Ask" or the "Tell"

- **G**ratitude
  Acknowledgements, thanking those who have contributed to the work

Along the way it is critical to emphasize the **key points**. Ultimately, what do you want the audience to take away? Assemble the evidence and clearly highlight in the allotted time. When technical data is used to make the point, it is important to share why that data is important. How was it generated? What are you comparing to? What is the data telling you?

And then there is the all-important **story**. It's what experts say provides a connection with the audience. Everybody can read the slides, but the story can serve as an "adhesive" that helps ideas stick with the audience. Numbers and templates can be easily forgotten. Stories can make it memorable, inform, and inspire. Stories don't have to be personal, it is about the storytelling and the narrative.

Once you have it all together, practice, rearrange, and re-organize as needed. Stay true to your style. Genuine authentic speakers are more successful in selling an idea or an ideology with their TALKS.

POINTS TO PONDER

What is the element that you find missing in most talks?

How are you integrating the story in your technical presentations?

Time Management
Giving You a Hard Time?

"Manage my time at work better." Let's be honest, how many people have resolved to do this at the beginning of a new year? Without a doubt, time management comes up as one of the most desired skills but also among the hardest to master. This is critical when lines on the to-do lists keep growing, deadlines are looming, and there is no lifeline in sight to help accomplish everything we need to do. So, how does one get organized to better manage time?

Three elements that are typically considered critical for effective time management include: awareness, arrangement, and adaptation.[39] Awareness requires that you think realistically about time as a limited resource. Arrangement focuses on organizing life's demands to effectively use time. Adaptation emphasizes the ongoing monitoring of how time is used, which includes adjusting to changing priorities. Time management is certainly a hot topic and came up at a group mentoring session at 3M. This gave me the opportunity to consider and share my strategies. My own system has evolved over time, and in examining it, I can see that the three elements yield positive outcomes when applied in concert with my evolving roles and personal philosophies. This includes customizing the approach to my working style.

TIME AFTER TIME

The key elements of my current time management philosophy include *everything, something, one thing, and nothing!* I have settled on a weekly rhythm where I do everything I can on my priority projects, something on the next tier priority, at least one thing to move along what I consider as a priority for future, and finally, always reserve blocks of nothing time. This is important, not just to serve as a buffer, but to carve out time for critical and creative thinking. My time management techniques have evolved to match my strategy for setting goals.

To keep the discipline, I commit to a status update, with team or stakeholders, to be issued at a predetermined cadence. Call it old-school, but the mode that works the best for me is a written communication. Compared with a casual oral summary, written correspondence can be difficult and feel time consuming, but I have found that formulating thoughts and putting them in writing forces one to crystallize what has

---

[39] Eric C. Dierdorff, "Time Management Is About More Than Life Hacks," Harvard Business Review, January 29, 2020.

happened, conclude what the progress means, and commit to what needs to be done next. As a result, I think it saves time in the long run. Besides being a great way to raise awareness, gain consensus, and solicit opinion from the team, it also helps build and steer the strategic narrative with key stakeholders on an ongoing basis.

For the top priorities, I follow a weekly cadence. Additional roles and responsibilities follow a biweekly or monthly reporting rhythm. This approach has sparked discussion around control of our time! How does one make time to do the work and write about it? It is indeed true that before we even start populating the calendar, we are pressed for time with the various meetings already on it which demand our attention. These may be corporate, functional, organizational, one-on-ones, reviews, updates, external speakers, committee meetings, mentoring, and networking, to name a few. One has to be judicious with planning attendance.

I have a few simple tactics I try to follow when committing to attend, and they work most of the time. I consider my role, importance, and engagement as I define for myself what constitutes prime time, face time, crunch time, and flex time.

- **Prime time** moments are the most important meetings given the primary goals, objectives, and priorities of a given role. These commitments are those that I must-attend. If a meeting or work trip is associated with top priorities, it is likely to require a lot of preparation. I try to block additional time ahead of these for preparation and pre-meetings as well as a post-meeting analysis.

- **Face time** decisions require that I take a hard look at which meetings I really need to attend, and those that I need to attend in person. Can I review the recording later? Can I delegate? Can I send an email update ahead of time and not attend? Can I read the minutes to get caught up? It's surprising how many times a quick five-minute phone-call, email, or text chat can eliminate a 30-minute meeting!

- **Crunch time** is defined by urgent meetings that are needed to resolve issues or make critical decisions. They require your presence and are bound to happen. These are also likely to throw the calendar in a tizzy. Is there a way to work them in early, late, or during the lunch hour? I have often taken urgent calls from mentees while eating, driving, or at home.

- **Flex time** is built in to allow for the inevitable and unpredictable demands of a given week. An important lesson from computer science is to avoid the costs of context switching, which are associated with the processing required to move from one task to another.[40] Much like a computer processor, our minds require resources to create space for new content and identify where we last were when returning to prior work. For this reason, it is key to save blocks of time for uninterrupted work in conjunction with flex time.

I zealously guard uninterrupted time, as it has become ever so important. It allows me to balance the need for flexibility in my calendar to accommodate external engagements, while accomplishing creative writing assignments that need me to stay focused on a single task for longer times. These strategies give me flexibility to make sure I can carve out what I call the ever-important **Tea(m) time** with mentees, committees, and peers.

ME-TIME

There are a myriad of tools and a multitude of techniques out there claiming to help people better manage their time. But, just like having a good brush doesn't make one a good artist, the handy hacks may not help to yield the desired results until they are personalized and internalized to match one's roles and goals at the time. In this age of constant connectivity, time management becomes extremely important. Otherwise, commitments can encroach deeply into *family-time*, *spare time*, and much needed *downtime*. On the other hand, connectivity also allows for some hacks to come in handy. I went for a walk while listening-in on a meeting, which allowed me to get my exercise in as well!

There are certainly times when I feel overwhelmed with everything that needs to get done – that's when it's list time! I take a pause to make a list. It allows me to process my thoughts and I feel unburdened in a way by putting it down on paper. I then start allocating each of the items on the list to the most appropriate "time zone" listed above. It gives me clarity on what needs to be addressed right away as well as assess the time each item may take and manage calendar accordingly.

There is no one-size-fits-all formula, but there is no time like the present to get started on different strategies and tactics. Just make sure to give them some... time.

POINTS TO PONDER

How have your time management skills evolved over time?

What are some tools, techniques, tips that you can personalize to save time?

---

[40] Samuel Flender, "The Science of Time Management," Towards Data Science, February 20, 2019.

Range!
The "IT Factor" for Innovation?

My name is Jayshree Seth, and I consider myself a generalist!

To be specific, this article started in an airport bookstore. I raced there as soon as my flight landed. My eyes couldn't keep up with my fingers, and my fingers couldn't keep up with my racing heart. The index finally came into focus: page 206. There it was:

"Jayshree Seth rose to corporate scientist precisely because she was allowed to pinball around different technology domains... She described her approach to innovation almost like investigative journalism...

'My inclination is to attack a problem by building a narrative.
I figure out the fundamental questions to ask... It's mosaic building.
I just keep putting those tiles together ...'" [41]

See, the previous night I had received some LinkedIn invitations from people who said they had read about me in a newly released book. I recalled a discussion with writer David Epstein, who was collecting data and interviewing people for a new book. It had been exciting to chat with someone who was convinced that the intense focus on specialization is a myth, apparently based on limited data. He argues that there's plenty of evidence to suggest that "range" is the true engine of innovation and creativity.

MAKE SOMETHING OF I.T.

Range: Why Generalists Triumph in a Specialized World, challenges conventional wisdom about what it takes to succeed. Epstein makes a very compelling case for generalization. He provides scientific data on education and professional excellence, showing that narrow specialization can lead to inflexibility of the thought-process required for innovation because one can get too steeped in convention to challenge intellectual norms. He gives examples from the history of *dabblers* who have managed to connect ideas from different fields, thereby profoundly impacting our world. He raises a question: Should everyone strive to be a generalist, a "T" to some degree?

---

[41] Jayshree Seth as quoted by David Epstein in Range: Why Generalists Triumph in a Specialized World

"I-shaped" and "T-shaped" are terms that apparently originated in reference to what kind of consultants to hire.[42] The "I" shape referred to individuals who were highly versed in a specific area of expertise and could drill deeper into a specific field. The "T" shape referred to those with expertise as well as broader skills and knowledge; they are individuals who can connect different perspectives from different fields. Epstein argues that people who don't have a strict plan dictating what they will be, or a narrow focus on a single interest, end up making amazing contributions because they can transfer knowledge from one field to another. Generalists understand concepts and see how these might apply to other areas, whereas specialists often have the risk of getting too entrenched in one set of facts such that they may "miss the forest for the trees".

The importance of T-shaped people is being highlighted more and more, given the pace of change, the business environment, and the heightened need for creativity and innovation, in light of global challenges. Many leaders have realized that T-people are distinctly better at seeking and fostering diverse connections that can bring innovative ideas to the table. There is a need to have a critical mass of T-shaped people, especially in today's seemingly hyper-specialized environments. In my view, it is imperative that any organization have a collective *range* that includes both *kinds* of people *and* a culture that brings them together for magic to happen. That is the real "IT factor"!

One way I see it, the I-*people can* **I**ndividually *solve problems*, but T-people may bring the unique skill to connect disparate information, *identify unique problems to solve*, and bring together cross-functional **T**eams to solve them creatively. In my case, working deep within the technical functions of 3M technology platforms with an amazing group of I-specialists, coupled with a strong culture of empowerment and collaboration, provided the real IT factor for success. We brought together the "I" and "T" effectively.

> *"T-people like myself can happily go to the I-people with questions to create the trunk for the T. Imagine me in a network where I didn't have the ability to access all these people. That really wouldn't work well..."* [41]

COUNT ON I.T.

Organizations should strive for this vector of diversity and the inclusion necessary to bring together I- and T-people to develop that range. Reward and recognition structures also need to be aligned to promote both styles. I-people individually can also develop T skills. Epstein, in fact, urges individuals (and parents) to abandon the desire for instant gratification and test-scores. He emphasizes the importance of traits

---

[42]Andy Boynton, "Are you an 'I' or a 'T'?" Forbes, October 18, 2011.

over particular skills, including curiosity and wonder, flexibility and open-mindedness, adventure-seeking, experiment-minded, and playfulness. These skills may be the key to creatively solving challenges which the world is counting on scientists to solve. In fact, 3M SOSI results generally reveal that people are very optimistic about the future of science and its potential to solve global problems.

David Epstein's book suggests that the way to succeed is by "sampling widely, gaining a breadth of experiences, taking detours, experimenting relentlessly, juggling many interests." Supplying the mind with lots of ideas allows it to make more connections, especially uncommon ones. We all need to strive to broaden our sources of information and knowledge, as a way of collecting dots to be able to connect them. What "it" takes is developing intellectual flexibility - in other words, developing range.

POINTS TO PONDER

What ways are you developing range for your own IT factor?

*How often do you interact or collaborate with people
who have different or complementary skill sets?*

LEAD In the Twilight Zone!
Between Reflection and Resolution...

The years feel like they fly by, and the New Year provides a necessary pause for reflection and subsequent resolution. It is a special time, the dusk of the year past and the impending dawn of the one just around the corner. Each year in my journey carries a different character, from those that fostered steady growth to those that were exhilarating in their change. As I grew in my career, a balance emerged between getting comfortable in my roles, yet stretching and developing further while managing a multitude of initiatives.

HOT AIR

In December 2018, I got to check off a bucket-list item: a hot air-balloon ride! I was impressed with the simplicity of the first, successful, human-carrying flight technology. Things have certainly come a long way since balloons made of paper and cloth rose with the smoke of burning straw and horse manure, but its significance was monumental at the time. At the outset, it was the keen observation, vision, and tenacity of a handful of people that made happen what was believed to be impossible.

The handful who had the **conviction and perseverance** to fulfill the human desire for flight. They reduced this challenge to practice, seemingly without any formal qualifications in science and engineering.

The ones who had the **vision and intuition** to understand the implications of their work. They promoted a culture that encouraged success and provided the resources and engagement to facilitate momentum.

And finally, those who subsequently contributed to these endeavors with scientific **discipline and detail**, accelerating the advancement of the technology.

COOL MOMENTS

These ideas have been reinforced as I have had the amazing opportunity to hear from some outstanding leaders and visionaries in recent years.

3M CEO, Mike Roman, set the tone of the 3M Leadership Conference in 2018 by focusing on people and performance. "Leadership –it's your job." We need to embrace change, and change is all around us. "One of the key tenets of leadership is facing reality." He specifically highlighted, along with focus on prioritization and execution, the importance of discipline and detail, which from my viewpoint is critical for engaged, knowledgeable leadership. I was particularly struck by how he models humility, a hallmark of good leaders.

Judson Althoff, Executive Vice President at Microsoft, shared his experiences relating to the company's transformation journey. He emphasized the importance of the company's vision and culture by the tone set at the top. His story-telling style was very powerful in communicating the narrative around listening to your customers and the importance of diverse perspectives. Their CEO Satya Nadella's quote, "It's better to be a learn-it-all than a know-it-all," really stood out for me as an example of driving a growth mindset.

Dr. Dambisa Moyo, 3M board member, author, and global economist, talked about the rapidly changing world and the fundamental shifts that are happening from virtually every standpoint: social, natural, demographic, technological, geopolitical, and the potential impact on economies and the way we do business today. It gave some good food for thought, as she questioned, "What do corporations have to do to survive in this era?"

It was an honor to be in the same room as a four star General! General Votel provided a military perspective on people and performance. The resounding parallels with corporations were clear: an emphasis on culture and empowerment of people is necessary so that "decisions can be made at the lowest competent level and risk is accepted at the highest accountable level."

Many messages were clearly applicable to everyone within an organization. *Make it personal; they are your customers. Make people and culture everyone's strategy.* These resonated with what I wrote in the above "Of Leaders and Ladders: Can you Lead Without Being 'The Boss'?" We can all try to take initiative, inform, influence, and inspire to have impact right from our rungs.

Dr. Mae Jemison, the first woman of color in space, gave an inspiring keynote at the Minnesota Governor's Council's 33rd Annual MLK Celebration. She eloquently summed up the imperative: "Science education and having more women and minority representation is key. We all have the talent, but we need all the perspectives."

All in all, given today's context it takes a vision and a village to *LEAD In: People, Work, and the Skill to Lead.*

> **L**istening and learning – practice, practice, practice

> **E**ngagement and empowerment – exercise it!

> **A**cceptance of change and risk acceptance – get comfortable with it

> **D**iversity AND Inclusion – be intentional

> **In**stinct and intuition – trust and train

COMFORT ZONE

Embracing these ideas throughout 2019 produced an incredible year. That December, I was able to reflect on my gratitude for the conferment of accolades that had come my way throughout the year, an affirmation of the path I was on. I grew comfortable in my roles yet stretching and developing further while managing a multitude of initiatives.

I felt like I got *in the zone* with our science advocacy efforts and the narrative that developed with my own story as a backdrop. I had the proud privilege to present internationally on the innovation culture at 3M and the results of 3M SOSI (State of Science Index). I engaged with a wide variety of audiences around the world: customers, thought-leaders, educators, students, and other stakeholders in the eco-system, urging them all to become strong advocates. It gave me utmost satisfaction to have the message resonate globally. The hospitality I experienced from hosts and 3Mers in Canada, Italy, India, Russia, and France was incredible.

I also had to step *outside my comfort zone*, though I thought I was already way outside! Out of my comfort zone and into a gown for the very first time, I presented the Recording Artist of the year at the JUNOS in Canada. I was interviewed live on Yahoo Finance with anchor Alexis Christoforous, and then alongside acclaimed broadcast journalist and media pioneer Katie Couric. I delivered the closing keynote at Society for Women Engineers Annual Meeting to more than 1,000 engineers. Finally, I represented 3M in our first major TV advertising campaign in over two decades, which was launched during the World Series. These new experiences certainly stretched me in different ways, and I am grateful for that.

I was around a lot of *flood the zone* activity as well, moving the needle on various ideas, inventions, and projects, as well as my additional roles at work. Being the 2019 Chair of our 3M Asian Employee Resource Network (A3CTION) was a unique opportunity for personal growth. A3CTION is one of our larger employee networks that brings together East Asians, South Asians, and Southeast Asians. Given the diversity within this group itself, diversity of the distinct cultures across the Asian diaspora, it became necessary to exercise "LEAD In" skills and focus the team on our similarities. To do this, we celebrated the common thread in our cultural heritages while educating the rest of the organization. We regularly conducted outreach events and company-wide communications, highlighting traditions and festivals that are so integral to the Asian cultural identity.

COLD HARD FACTS

Given all these commitments, there were certainly times where it felt like a *war zone*, but we navigated through it. The pace of the year required the patience, guidance, and support of my village: my managers, teams, collaborators, my friends, and family. The success of each individual is often determined by the people around them, the people who adjust, compromise, and encourage you on your journey of personal and professional growth. I reflect on this aspect and the acknowledgment is an exercise in gratitude. It's a reflection in the *quiet zone* every year that I resolve to continue to do.

POINTS TO PONDER

How do you capture your reflections from the year past?

*How do you carry what you've learned
in the past year into the coming year?*

Work that 2020 Vision:
Light! Camera! Action!

At the beginning of a new decade, 2020 gave us a great tagline. After all, who hadn't heard a reference to "20/20 vision" in the context of the year? The phrase motivated us with a powerful metaphor, signifying sharpness of focus and clarity of action. With 20/20 vision, you have normal visual acuity. This means you can see anything that should *normally* be seen at a distance of 20 feet. So, how can this metaphor help us plan for the future and attain our goals with wisdom, creativity, and imagination?

Although it refers to normal vision, nothing extraordinary, the metaphor has something more to offer us than what meets the eye! Maybe it can inspire us to effectively achieve our goals and resolutions with a clear action plan. Let's examine this further, scientifically. When we look at an object, light from that object strikes the lens of the eye and an upside-down image of that object is formed on the retina, a light-sensing structure inside the eye.[43] This captured image is sent from the retina, along the optic nerve, to the visual cortex in the brain where it is interpreted as the upright image of the object. The brain either files the information for future reference, or it sends a message to a motor area if any movement is warranted. Vision is ultimately about the receipt of information, its communication and interpretation, and the action it evokes.

HOW EYE SEE IT

The eye accomplishes this with a series of highly functional structures that collaborate seamlessly and efficiently to facilitate the chemical changes and electrical impulses needed to control three key factors that take us from perception to action. These three factors are: 1. How accurately the cornea and lens focus the *light* coming into the eye onto the retina; 2. The ability of the nerves in the retina to capture the image like a *camera* and send it to the visual cortex in the brain; and finally 3. The ability of the brain to interpret the image and initiate *action* based on what is being seen (and felt by the other senses), telling the body what to do with the information received from the eyes.

The onset of a year signals a sharper focus on the future and compels us to see everything clearly. It is the voice of the director cueing our entrance. Here are a few ways we can perhaps enhance our focus and cognition for successful execution.

---

[43] Kellogg Eye Center, "Anatomy of the Eye," University of Michigan Medicine

The way vision works can inspire us to work our vision, to achieve the goals we set forth for us and our people, or as leaders in our organizations. Vision starts with the right framework or structure, aligned with a keen eye towards prioritization, focus, and execution for *light, camera, action!*

- **Light**

  Light is what enters the eye and ultimately gets captured on the retina. Once the light enters the system, a lot of the sub-systems are engaged in its processing. So, it is important to determine: Do we have the right field of view with the right frame of reference? Is our perspective consistent with the lens of our strategic goals and **priorities**? Are we oriented in the right direction and looking at what is important to look at? Do we all see the light?

- **Camera**

  Recording the image and sending it on to the brain is the basis of communication. It is critical to have a sharp **focus** for the brain to be able to interpret what is being seen. What filters and lenses are being used to constitute a focused image? How are the inner workings of the system operating? How efficiently is the information that came in being captured, gathered, and communicated? Are any blind spots getting in the way of transmitting an accurate picture?

- **Action**

  Action is about cognition, interpreting the information in the visual cortex to facilitate a response. The brain will also integrate other inputs, alongside vision, such as from sensory and motor stimuli to determine course of action. Do we have all the other necessary systems working well? And are they working in unison such that **execution** of action will have the desired impact? Do we truly have our eye on the ball?

KEEP AN EYE OUT

The metaphor can be extended further. 20/20 vision only indicates sharpness or clarity of sight from a distance. It does not account for other critical attributes that affect vision, such as peripheral awareness or side vision, eye coordination, perception of depth, ability to focus, or the ability to perceive color. As we execute towards our goals: *Do we have the peripheral awareness of what is going on at the very edges? How can it derail or disrupt our ultimate vision? Are we able to perceive how imminent a threat is? Do we have the right coordination and collaboration to act with agility if warranted? Can we do that with heightened focus on priorities in a sustained manner? And finally, are we able to see things for what they truly are, multifaceted, in all its depth, with all their colors?*

Our eyes function as the primary connection between the outside world and the world within us. The way we respond, react, and reflect is strongly associated with our vision. Eyes allow us to see but even our subconscious is impacted by the sense of sight, as our dreams are visual.

Let's dream big. The eyes of the world are on us. Light, camera, action!

POINTS TO PONDER

What strategies do you use to bring broader vision in focus?

What elements do you often need to correct to achieve successful execution?

PRACTICE:
Exercising That Leadership Muscle

What kind of a leader would you be if you were thrust into chaos or crisis?
We are all living through a truly historic challenge of epic proportion. New and
situational leaders are emerging, and the leadership capacity of many is being tested.
Very often, the unpredictable nature of such events can put one's decision-making
process and skills to test. Given that, it is always good to experience situations where
one has to make decisions or recommendations under pressure, with limitations such
as a stringent timeline, minimal resources, or even no clear authority. These experiences,
often outside the comfort zone, make for good practice. I feel fortunate to have
had opportunity to exercise that leadership muscle as a "game-changer" in 3M's
prestigious Catalyst Leadership Development program.

The Catalyst Leadership Development program includes classroom activities,
360 assessments, one-on-one coaching, engaging with thought-leaders, such as CEOs
and board members, and experiential learning through expertise-based projects in
communities around the world. The goal is to make a positive impact for 3M and
the global communities where we work and live. To this end, 3M game-changers
have partnered with non-profit organizations and social enterprises in communities
throughout the USA, India, China, Morocco, and Costa Rica to tackle some of
the world's most pressing challenges related to climate change, circular economy,
healthcare, and education. I had the unique opportunity to be part of the contingent
working with non-profits in Ghana, while others in our cohort partnered with local
organizations in Ukraine and Peru.

GAME-CHANGERS

Our team of four, comprised of a marketing leader, business leader, R&D
management leader, and myself as a technical leader, partnered with Safe Water
Network (SWN), a non-profit engaged in providing safe, affordable, and reliable
water to rural and peri-urban, under-served communities in Ghana. It was incredibly
inspiring to interact with the SWN folks who were so committed to their mission
and passionate about their organization's goals. Their involvement and effort made
our visit educational and meaningful. Working with constrained resources forced
us to think creatively and challenge the return on investment of every idea as we
developed our recommendation.

In looking back, it was a unique opportunity to not only hone leadership skills, but also develop a broader perspective, exercise creative thinking, and build network, all while positively contributing to global issues and sustainable development goals. Personally, volunteering time and talent to make a difference and contributing to a larger purpose was very rewarding. It allowed me to learn from my peers and use skills that I don't use often to contribute to ideas that are not relevant to my functional background, expertise, or roles.

PERFECTING THE GAME

It was very rewarding to see the positive response to our team's recommendations for addressing some key challenges faced by SWN. Looking back, I believe there were several elements, outlined below, that made for a successful partnership and well-received final outcome. These included the *pre-work, field work, and teamwork*. All in all, I feel honored, grateful, and glad to have had this leadership PRACTICE!

- **P**roblem-to-solve

  It was critical to collectively agree on what problem(s) we would focus on as a team during our time in Ghana and frame the statement of work around this primary priority. We had incredible partnership with SWN and facilitation by coaches from 3M and Pyxera Global to get us to this crucial point via phone-calls and emails.

- **R**esearch

  Since all of us on the team had limited understanding and exposure to water-related business and technology, we all took some time to augment our knowledge with secondary research, including discussions with 3M and other global experts in the area. This helped in getting a baseline of understanding as we prepared for primary research.

- **A**nalytics

  When in Ghana we went through a process of inquiry to further our understanding after meeting with key stakeholders in the partner organization. The pre-work helped in asking the right questions of the right people and examining all the data available to start forming the hypothesis based on our preliminary assessment.

- Comprehensive view

  As is the case with any challenge, it is imperative to get a 360 view of the challenge at hand. In this case, it came from the field-visits, meeting personnel on the frontlines, and input from the rural and peri-urban customers as well as other stakeholders in the process. This helped with logistical as well as holistic understanding.

- Team-time

  Throughout the process we were formulating our thoughts individually, so it was critical to have several team "downloads" where we talked about our observations and key takeaways with each other, which included the perspectives of our functional expertise. This was very valuable to form the backdrop for our evolving recommendations and consensus.

- Ideation

  The process towards development of our final recommendations followed quite organically given the ongoing discussions, hard data, gut instinct, and intuition. At a high level, we followed a methodology I have devised, and use often to consolidate thoughts into categories, "The now, the new, the wow, and the how."

- Communication

  Once we gelled on our recommendations, effort was dedicated to frame them with adequate context and deliver with credibility. This was important, since a few of our recommendations were bound to stretch SWN. We needed to paint a vision and a path for the organization to be able to get there. Given that, we used data, examples, analogies, and parallels.

- Empathy

  A critical motivation behind our effort and the ever-present element in the entire process, empathy went a long way in building trust within the team, with our partner organization, and in the field. Our leadership coaches also reminded us to have empathy towards ourselves as we worked well outside of our comfort zone.

I feel blessed to have had this opportunity, on many counts. I am grateful for the intense practice in crystallizing a problem, researching a new area, analyzing data, interacting with stakeholders, and formulating ideas with the team that could be communicated with the desired impact. The two weeks were also a great practice for the ability to empathize, which certainly is a hallmark of leadership.

The more we train and the more we practice, the stronger the leadership muscle gets so it can take command, with consistency and confidence, in times of chaos and crisis. Perfection, in leadership or anything else for that matter, is not a destination, it's a journey. Practice can be a trusted companion.

POINTS TO PONDER

What works well for your leadership PRACTICE?

How are you finding opportunities for yourself to PRACTICE leadership skills?

SECTION 4

Thought Leadership
On the Need for Developing a Growth Context

"...[L]ove challenges, be intrigued by mistakes, enjoy effort, and keep on learning."

—Carol Dweck, Author of Mindset

SUCCESS...
In the Time of Pandemic

Certainly, 2020 did not shape up the way any of us would have envisioned. Whatever vision metaphor we may have started the year with, the pandemic slapped a new lens on our "VUCA World". An acronym borrowed from the military,[44] VUCA has been often used to describe the business environment as well. In a world that is constantly changing and frequently unfolding in unexpected ways, business is *volatile*. It is difficult to anticipate or predict events through our past experiences rendering situations and scenarios very *uncertain*. Most of these challenges are multifaceted and interlinked, making them *complex*. Often, they are contradictory and paradoxical, adding to the *ambiguity*.

HINDSIGHT

Considering how much changed in such a short period of time, the COVID-19 pandemic made the prior VUCA World look quite tame and manageable! In a pandemic world, the discussion of **vulnerability** eclipsed any discussion of volatility. Vulnerability was exposed, not just as it related to our health, but to our communities, companies, and countries. The crisis brought into focus the crucial connections between human health, the environment, and the economy with the vulnerability of virtually every sector: financial, healthcare, education, manufacturing, and the list goes on.

It is difficult to overstate the significance of the transitions brought on by the pandemic throughout 2020, and impossible to predict the major shifts that are yet on the horizon. The pandemic impacted the very way we lived and the way we worked. The world was largely unprepared for what transpired, even though in hindsight, it was not entirely unexpected. Much has been said about the cognitive bias of hindsight,[45] that is, the tendency to view events as more likely to have occurred after they occur than before. But in modern history, the pandemic was **unprecedented**. Indeed, it was unprecedented in its wide-ranging impact and the preparedness in dealing with it.

The debate of lives versus livelihoods raged on as we shifted to meet the new normal. Whether the optimal approach was as objective as "flattening the curve" or "social distancing", all subjects were deemed controversial. Instead of being discussed,

---

[44] VUCA World, https://www.vuca-world.org/
[45] Mark Travers, "Were People Worried About a Pandemic Before COVID-19? Hardly, According to a Study of Global Attitudes," Forbes, March 24, 2020.

it often appeared that strategies were disputed, heightening deep rooted issues within societies while pitting people and ideologies against each other. Complex gave way to **contentious**. Especially since social media served to amplify many of the issues such as rampant misinformation during this pandemic. Every action, the words, and the abundant rhetoric was **amplified**, constantly leading to additional challenges for individuals, leaders, corporations, and organizations. It appeared that in the rough season of this new viral VUCA World, only a few could navigate successfully.

FORESIGHT

I had the opportunity to discuss innovation as it relates to the pandemic environment, where I shared my take on VUCA. We talked about why some entities were able to adjust, pivot, or adapt more quickly than others, including how leadership and vision, as well as a culture and mindset of innovation,[46] are central to this capability. As an example, 3M was able to secure its supply chain and double production of N95 masks while establishing leave policies and robust protocols to ensure employee support and safety. Product was redirected to where it was most needed to provide solutions, while also fighting price gouging and fraud, by working cooperatively with government and collaboratively with other companies. In addition, CEO Mike Roman announced a $20 million donation to support health care workers, COVID-19 research, and communities disproportionately impacted by the pandemic. "It's important that 3M holds true to its core values during this pandemic by supporting our communities and improving lives," he said in a statement.[47]

In 2019, many CEOs signed the Statement on the Purpose of a Corporation.[48] The one-page declaration ends as follows: *"Each of our stakeholders is essential. We commit to deliver value to all of them, for the future success of our companies, our communities and our country."* This included a much-needed shift from shareholder value to stakeholder capitalism for long-term value. It is inspiring to be at a company whose CEO has signed on to be a part of the legacy of shared prosperity, and sustainability, for both business and society.

INSIGHT

In the context of economic recovery, the pandemic provided moments for companies to put their commitment to stakeholder capitalism[49] into practice, as VUCA took on a new perspective:

---

[46] MH&L Staff, "What's the Secret of Companies Able to Pivot Supply Chains During Pandemic?" Material Handling & Logistics, April 28, 2020.
[47] "3M continues fight against COVID-19 with aid for U.S., global relief and recovery efforts," 3M News Center, April 16, 2020.
[48] "Business Roundtable Redefines the Purpose of a Corporation to Promote 'An Economy That Serves All Americans'," Business Roundtable, August 19, 2020.
[49] Alison Omens, "How To Be A Stakeholder-Driven Company In A Pandemic," Forbes, March 12, 2020.

Volatility	→	**V**ulnerability
Uncertainty	→	**U**nprecedented
Complex	→	**C**ontentious
Ambiguous	→	**A**mplified

Although VUCA may have evolved throughout the pandemic, the fundamentals of a multi-stakeholder model didn't change. If anything, the pandemic may have served as the catalyst to further heighten focus on authentic compassion for employees, care for customers and suppliers, and concern for society and sustainability, leading us into a new era of value creation. Throughout the stages of "infinite present", the pandemic accelerated the relevance of the multi-stakeholder model as an idea whose time had already come. Innovation must be directed primarily towards significance moving forward. Otherwise, those with continued focus on traditional metrics may be blindsided.

The approach that will spell SUCCESS:

Significance that

Underscores

Customers

Communities

Employees

Shareholders

Suppliers

As leading futurist Daniel Burrus said, "So instead of success being the goal, significance is the goal, success is one of the after elements of being significant." [50]

POINTS TO PONDER

What are you or your organization doing differently as a result of the shifting paradigms associated with the 2020 pandemic?

How has your definition of success evolved during these heightened VUCA times?

---

[50] Neil C. Hughes, "1149: Daniel Burrus, Managing Uncertainty Caused by COVID-19," The Tech Blog Writer, March 22, 2020.

Got CHANGE?
Penny for Your Thoughts...

"Change, the only constant," was a well-accepted adage even in pre-COVID days, but as we lived through unprecedented VUCA times (Volatile, Uncertain, Complex, Ambiguous), there was a change even in the nature of change. Some have called 2020 a "punctuated equilibrium",[51] a term used in one of the theories of evolution referring to periods when there is tremendous change after a long period of stability. What happens in this punctuated equilibrium is change, lots of change, and very fast.

One can see why the evolutionary parallel was drawn to the times when the pandemic raged and why we often struggled to make sense of it all. It's not just that multiple crises unfolded, but the rapid transformation that accompanied them with the recognition that our systems and our mindsets are built for gradual, continuous improvement. Moreover, there was the realization that this change, and the very nature of change, required a very different stance. There was no playbook to guide us; we were back to the workbooks! All of us became students, in all humility, constantly learning new vocabulary, assimilating new information, and finding new ways of working and living. Virtually all of humanity had this experience: facing the same threats, confronting the same fears, and *awaiting the same gift of science.*

UNABRIDGED

We grieve for those severely impacted by the pandemic and its fallout, finding ourselves also mourning the loss of normalcy and lack of control, as it influenced almost all aspects of our lives. While we lived through the seemingly "infinite present", we missed milestones, many events and trips, and meeting friends, family, and colleagues. Despondent thoughts were further compounded with the multiplicity of crises, such as the intractable virus of racism and the worsening economic outlook. We worried and we worry. While we wait for a vaccine, we worry for ourselves, our loved ones, and the future. Everyone seems to have gone through some cycle of grief in the punctuated equilibrium that was 2020. Thoughts of denial, shock, numbness, anger, fear, panic, guilt, gratitude, and hope...and then the intense desire to help and be productive, with mindfulness, with purpose.

---

[51] William F. Meehan III, "Jim Coulter Of TPG: Leadership When Change is Changing," Forbes, July 15, 2020.

When I look back, I can't help but think that my pre-COVID days in 2020 were perhaps foretelling of the future. My year started with an inspiring 20/20 vision, some key time management strategies and an amazing opportunity to practice my leadership muscle through a community service project. When the pandemic hit, it brought about a lot of change, virtually altering the definition of success in many ways.

But my experiences in early 2020 guided me to pivot, prioritize, and be productive with focus and execution on helping in any way I could. The many fellow 3Mers who rallied in the fight against the pandemic were truly inspirational for all of us. Further work included advancing membrane technology for biopharma filtration solutions supporting new vaccine and therapeutic development efforts. We also expanded partnerships, including development of new innovative rapid diagnostic COVID-19 tests with the Massachusetts Institute of Technology.

I was fortunate to be able to work from home and also continue teaching, coaching, and mentoring activities virtually. In addition to project work I was able to maintain science advocacy efforts, which also transitioned to virtual mode: webinars, panels, and presentations. Virtually, I participated in events with summer interns and STEM camps. It was exciting to launch 3M Science at Home to help teachers, parents, and students with distance-learning. And when the intractable virus of racism was exposed, learning about the issues at hand was key in committing to take steps to become an anti-racist and impact change.

BRIDGING STRATEGY

The story of the Choluteca Bridge is one that resonates in the midst of this change. It's the extraordinarily strong, stable, engineering marvel in Honduras, built in 1996. When Hurricane Mitch ravaged the region, everything was destroyed except for the bridge. The flooding forced the river itself to change course, literally rendering it a bridge to nowhere with no river flowing under it. The lesson in this true story is very relevant and has recently been circulating on social media because of the level of change we are seeing in the world.

I too had an opportunity to share this as a metaphor for change at a 3M Technical Forum event in August 2020, hosted by our Technical Leadership chapter. From a leadership perspective, the rapid change around us requires courage to view the challenges posed by the sea change as an opportunity. I described three distinct actions we can all take.

First, are the opportunities to anticipate the "new normal" given the acceleration of many trends and develop *actionable insight* to execute new strategies rapidly in the short-term. Decisions that may have seemed strategic from a long-term perspective may require more immediate action to stay relevant as change accelerates.

Second, this change also calls for *honest* soul-searching since the pandemic has revealed vulnerabilities, strengths, and shortcomings. Such reflection can, in fact, lead to *strategic foresight* by challenging "old truths". Shifting paradigms warrant *humility* and acceptance, as the proverbial river may have changed course in this period of rapid change. This provides an opportunity to examine if we are *adapting*, what we are learning, and convey how we are adjusting our future plans as a result.

Finally, there is no doubt in my mind that science will vanquish the pandemic. This punctuated equilibrium, this brief "window of time", behooves us to change things within our *operational oversight* that don't work well for us and streamline and simplify processes that help us add value. We all need to keep a growth mindset and build *grit*, resilience, and flexibility.

So, what's next? More *change*. It's coming. We need to bridge to the future. It is imperative for leaders to maintain neutrality and transparency in communications, balanced with pragmatic optimism, lest *negativity* leads to a sense of hopelessness.

We all lead change. Our thoughts and actions can inspire and empower us to navigate change with:

> **C**ourage
>
> **H**onesty and humility
>
> **A**dapting: attitude, altitude
>
> **N**eutrality, not negativity
>
> **G**rowth through grit
>
> **E**xpect more CHANGE

In this time of rapid change, during the height of the pandemic, the irony wasn't lost on me when I heard about a coin shortage... a shortage of change.

POINTS TO PONDER

*What helped you deal with the sudden
and rapid CHANGE in 2020?*

*What did this experience reveal
to you about yourself?*

"So, let us not be blind to our differences. But let us also direct attention to our common interests and to the means by which those differences can be resolved. And if we cannot end now our differences, at least we can help make the world safe for diversity. For, in the final analysis, our most basic common link is that we all inhabit this small planet. We all breathe the same air. We all cherish our children's future. And we are all mortal." [52]

—U.S. President John F. Kennedy

----

[52] "We all breathe the same air," speech, Washington, D.C., June 10, 1963.

Race to Cure:
Going Antiviral...

We may breathe the same air, but some breathe less freely. We see that some are filled with dread every day for their children and that systemic racism has conspired against some to have more frequent encounters with mortality. It has also become evident that those of us who see ourselves as colorblind, and thus fair, must change. The time has come "not to be blind to our differences."

A VIRUS AND THE VIRUS

The deaths of George Floyd and Breonna Taylor at the hands of police have really brought into heightened focus the pervasive and out-of-control nature of the virus that is racism. Just like COVID-19, racism has infected many, spreads uncontrollably, and too often kills. It turns skin color into a comorbidity factor. However, unlike COVID-19, there is no vaccine we can develop to eventually eradicate it. We will have to collectively figure out how to purge this insidious virus which has plagued our systems for many centuries.

While the intersection of these two viruses convulsed our nation, it also served to bring the impact of racism into focus. Many medical professionals currently overwhelmed with the plight of black and brown coronavirus patients have called racism a public health crisis.[53] They have committed to stand with protestors in absolute solidarity for the belief that racism, unless eradicated, will always be a greater threat to justice than the coronavirus. A post-pandemic America would nevertheless remain sick. As Dr. Arjun Arya instructs, "Yes, wear a mask. Yes, do your best to maintain distance. Yes, wash your hands. And yes, absolutely yes, join your allies to abolish injustice."[54]

Science education and STEM fields are also impacted by the racism virus.[55] We need all the diversity of thoughts and experiences we can get in order to creatively solve the problems we face and to unlock the secrets to a sustainable future. STEM professionals and academics have a huge influence on shaping the world. However,

---

[53] Divya Seth, "Medicine vs. racism: White coats for Black lives," KevinMD, June 3, 2020.
[54] Arjun Arya, "I'm a doctor in Minneapolis treating coronavirus patients. Until racism is abolished, it will always be a greater threat to justice than this virus," Business Insider, June 4, 2020.
[55] Siobhan Neela-Stock, "Scientists strike to call out systemic racism in STEM," Mashable, June 10, 2020.

of all the scientists and engineers in the United States, only three percent are black men and just two percent are black women, according to the National Science Foundation.[56]

VIRAL V.U.C.A. WORLD

The coronavirus pandemic slapped a new lens on our VUCA world. Bill George, ex-CEO of Medtronic, suggested that VUCA evolve from its traditional military elements of volatility, uncertainty, complexity, and ambiguity into VUCA 2.0, describing authentic leadership elements of vision, understanding, courage, and adaptability.[57] A pandemic-oriented VUCA world required another transformation, what I called a viral VUCA, a 3.0 iteration: vulnerability, unprecedented, contentious, and amplified.[58]

With the exposed onslaught of this intractable racism pandemic it is perhaps time for VUCA 4.0 as we move forward. In my view, we need to reflect upon our **values** as a nation, community, and at a personal level. We need to educate ourselves on the trauma caused by this virus, empathize with those most affected, and stand in **unity** against it. We need **commitment** to action, to "start where you are, use what you have, do what you can." [59] And all of this begins with **acknowledgment** of the problems.

We agree that silence is complicity. We accept that it may be awkward. We may make mistakes, but we move forward, mindful of **VUCA 4.0: Values, Unity, Commitment, Acknowledgment.**

At 3M, Chief Executive Officer Mike Roman and Chief Diversity Officer Ann Anaya convened a virtual "Candid Conversation" as a first response to listen and deepen understanding of the tragedy in our backyard. Thousands listened as diverse leaders across 3M shared perspectives, personal experiences, and optimism that we will move to action, united in solidarity. It was emotional and inspirational, reinforcing the commitment to become anti-racist.

PERSONAL IMMUNITY

On a personal level, I feel the urgency of the moment and have been educating myself on structural, or systemic, racism. Reading, reflecting, and ruminating has helped to detect my own conditioning, identify my own pockets of privilege, and use a growth mindset to plan my action steps. My children and their friends have been instrumental in shaping my thinking, teaching me that silence is complicity.[60] They have educated me on the folly and danger of a colorblind mentality. If I claim to care for equality,

---

[56] National Science Foundation, National Center for Science and Engineering Statistics, 2019. "Women, Minorities, and Persons with Disabilities in Science and Engineering: 2019."
[57] Bill George, "VUCA 2.0: A Strategy for Steady Leadership in an Unsteady World," Forbes, February 17, 2017.
[58] Jayshree Seth, "Success...in the time of pandemic", ThisBook, pg...
[59] Quote by Arthur Ashe
[60] Suparna Malia, "You're Complicit in This Racist System if You're Not Outraged," American Kahani, June 2, 2020.

I cannot be blind to inequality, cannot ignore the *headwinds* and *tailwinds* people experience and how that shapes their lives and narratives.

Our daughter, in fact, came to me and my husband with a sign she had painted to support Black Lives Matter, asking to put it in the front yard. Our first instincts were fearful, "No, you can't!"

"If you really care about BLM, why are you afraid of the sign?" she asked.

Suddenly, we were confronted with our fear. We live in a predominantly white, suburban neighborhood. I was afraid of this act changing the balance in life we had worked hard to create. Afraid of perceptions and fearful of repercussions. Though we had supported our children as they marched in protests, it made me realize that we had not resolved the tension we felt about our own involvement.

Within my peer group of South Asian immigrants, our American children have highlighted not only our fear, but the privilege associated with longstanding allyship with mainstream society that we didn't even understand. Privilege is a self-serving strategy that was seemingly compatible with our cultural norms. We are Indian immigrants, raised with a mindset that perhaps encouraged us to align with the meritocratic culture. This led to success and status with a "model minority" stereotype that is perhaps as confining as it is empowering.

I think of this transition into awareness much like any existing phenomenon that we come to understand as we have words to describe it. Consider the novelty of a "polar vortex", the way the term gripped the news cycle in 2014. Having never heard those two words combined, the concept was novel to the general public because it did not exist in our mainstream vocabulary. Rationally, the first time we learned about a polar vortex wasn't the first time it existed, as meteorologists will be happy to tell you. So, too, racism has existed in the United States though our collective vocabulary was limited. Listening to young South Asian voices name the connection between acts of violence and systemic racism provided the vocabulary I needed. South Asians understand racism and colorism in our own history, including the impacts of Imperial rule.

MITIGATION MEASURES

Our kids have shown us that we've allowed our immigrant status to distance ourselves from the fabric of what's happening across the nation. My training as a scientist and engineer enabled me to accept this new information, hard as it was to realize that I might be part of the problem. After all, we're taught to look at the information before us, understand our assumptions, and test our ideas to reach a conclusion. In the midst of such overwhelming evidence, it is impossible to ignore the impact of racism in American society.

Just because I could look at it from an intellectual perspective doesn't eliminate the emotional side of this story. I felt guilt that it had taken me so long to name what has existed, and the process of understanding was painful. I had to take time to reconcile how I felt about myself. Because of the distancing required by the pandemic, I had ample time to really consider what had happened and who I wanted to be in the midst of it all.

How many things happen all around us that we don't have the time or presence of mind to really explore? As scientists and engineers, we understand the importance of informed citizens, but there are many aspects of academic and corporate culture that outpace our ability to be the informed citizens we seek.

My desire is to move forward in a progressive way that is good for humanity. Once I truly understood what my daughter was telling me, I had to do something about it. I have started following people who are well-informed on the topic and amplifying their voices. Many books, raw and revealing articles, podcasts, and heartbreaking statements of personal experiences have helped in understanding the situation and my own feelings, fueling the intense desire to act. One of the books that really spoke to me, and helped frame and reframe my thinking, is *The Person You Mean to Be* by NYU Stern Professor Dolly Chugh.[61] It helps one understand bias and how to use "ordinary privilege" to stand up against injustice while making the world and ourselves better. We need to stand firmly in a position of anti-racism. "Neutrality kills." [62]

ANTIVIRAL

Structural racism refers to the totality of ways in which societies foster racial discrimination through mutually reinforcing systems of housing, education, employment, earnings, benefits, credit, media, health care, and criminal justice.[63] Science-based research has shown that when majority groups stay quiet, they inadvertently license the oppression of marginalized groups.[64] In fact, those with power and privilege actually have an easier time getting heard. We all need to acknowledge, affirm, and act to take steps to combat racism and become anti-racists.[65]

Racism is indeed a virus, and much like COVID-19, it spreads but it can appear asymptomatic. We have to call attention to it and isolate its carriers. Only then can we attempt containment.

---

[61] Dolly Chugh, The Person You Mean to Be: How Good People Fight Bias
[62] Cy Wakeman, "How I'm Committing To Evolve," Reality Based Leadership, June 4, 2020.
[63] Bailey et al., 2017. "Structural racism and health inequities in the USA: evidence and interventions," The Lancet.
[64] Adam Grant, "Why White People Stay Silent on Racism, and What to Read First," Microsoft News, June 7, 2020.
[65] Morgan Roberts and Washington, "U.S. Businesses Must Take Meaningful Action Against Racism," Harvard Business Review, June 1, 2020.

This virus, with no vaccine, warrants strong antiviral measures to be cured:

- **Do not MASK it.**
  - — Expose it within yourself and anywhere you see it
- **Promote SOCIAL CONVERGING**
  - — Unify your personal and professional stance
- **We must not WASH OUR HANDS of it**
  - — Embrace this matter because it impacts us all

And yes, absolutely yes, let's join our allies to abolish injustice.

POINTS TO PONDER

*How did you educate yourself or others
around you about systemic racism?*

What steps can you take to commit to social justice?

*"One of the great liabilities of history is that all too many people
fail to remain awake through great periods of social change.
Every society has its protectors of status quo and its fraternities
of the indifferent who are notorious for sleeping through revolutions.
Today, our very survival depends on our ability to stay awake,
to adjust to new ideas, to remain vigilant
and to face the challenge of change."* [66]

—**Martin Luther King Jr.**

---

[66]Where Do We Go from Here: Chaos or Community? (Beacon Press, 1968).

WorldSkills!
SKILLS for the Future World?

What are the "right" skills for the future in our rapidly changing world? I had the incredible opportunity to attend the 45th WorldSkills Competition in Kazan, Russia. The competition included 1,354 competitors, 63 countries and regions, 56 skills, and 4 days of intense events. Alongside the competition, a WorldSkills Conference was held to discuss this and other pressing questions for the sector including: How can an agile generation of skilled young people be trained for the future? How will they stay relevant in the face of economic, social, and technological transformations? What are the skills missing in your industry? How can we collaborate to find solutions to close the skills gap?

The conference was attended by industry leaders, policymakers, education and training providers, researchers, and change-makers from around the globe. It served as an international incubator for innovative solutions for change. In addition to participating in a panel on gender-balance titled "No women? No success for the 4th Industrial Revolution", I gave the keynote for a session titled "Skills for the future". In this rapidly evolving technological and digital world, adopting and maintaining the "right" skills can often feel like an impossible task. The keynote was followed by a workshop to explore new ways to train the workforce to better adapt to our evolving economies.

SKILLFUL WORDS

I talked about the "right" *skills*, or rather the mindset, that will be necessary for work in the future, taking inspiration from some quotable quotes you can't argue with! So, what are they?

The "right" skill is to be able to train your mind to see uncommon connections and build on them. Study the **science of art and art of science**, as many critical advancements that will shape our landscape will be at the confluence of different fields and will require breakdown of traditional thinking and silos.

> *"Principles for the development of a complete mind: Study the science of art.*
> *Study the art of science. Develop your senses – especially learn how to see.*
> *Realize that everything connects to everything else."*
>
> — **Leonardo da Vinci,** Italian Polymath of Renaissance Period

The "right" skill is to be able to strike a balance between knowledge and experience, to advance learning. These skills are about **know-how and knowledge**. Gain "knowledge", the facts, and information. Master "know-how", the knowledge of how to do something.

> *"The interaction of knowledge and skills with experience is key to learning."*
>
> — **John Dewey,** American Philosopher and Educational Reformer

The "right" skill is to consistently exercise **individual initiative**. Initiative is the imperative for innovation, imagination, and inspiration. It often starts with the motivation, drive, and vision of a single person to work hard to achieve something.

> *"Success depends in a very large measure upon individual; initiative and exertion, and cannot be achieved except by a dint of hard work."*
>
> — **Anna Pavlova,** Russian Prima Ballerina

The "right" skill is to be able to commit to **life-long learning**. This requires learning, unlearning, relearning. It's about recognizing and accepting that change is the only constant.

> *"The illiterate of the 21st century will not be those who cannot read and write, but who cannot learn, unlearn and relearn."*
>
> — **Alvin Toffler,** American Writer and Futurist
> *(Known for his works discussing modern technologies.)*

The "right" skill involves feeling empowered to take action and influencing others to do the same. Empowerment is about **leading from your own rung**. You don't have to climb to the top of the ladder to lead.

> *"If your actions inspire others to dream more, learn more, do more and become more, you are a leader."*
>
> — **John Quincy Adams,** American Statesman, Sixth President of the United States

The "right" skill is to never forget the human element in all we do. The human element is about **society and sustainability**. About seeing the "big picture" through a lens of humanity in all its diversity...and its unity.

> *"What's the real shtick? It's SHTEM! Science, Humanities, Technology, Engineering and Math."*
>
> — **Jayshree Seth,** Corporate Scientist and Chief Science Advocate

So here they are, the word SKILLS in my view that spell the "right" skills for the world of the future:

Studying art of science and science of art

Know-how and knowledge

Individual initiative

Learning, unlearning, relearning

Leading from your rung

Society and Sustainability in the forefront

The application of science, advancement of skills, and empowerment of diverse talent is key to a sustainable future as we face unprecedented challenges and opportunity. Did I get it "right"?

POINTS TO PONDER

What do you believe are the "right" skills for the #FutureOfWork?

What steps can we all take to continually building the "right" skills?

Confidence Rap[67]

I won't fake it...'coz I can't take it!
It's all about ACTION...
...and I know I can make it!!

---

[67]Written by Jayshree Seth for the 2019 "Celebrate SWE!" Closing Keynote at the Society of Women Engineers' Annual Conference

Minding the Confidence Gap?
It's a Rap!

When was the first time you were exposed to the concept of confidence? Was it a classmate who boldly raised their hand and asked questions? Was it a teammate whose belief in winning inspired you? Or were you applauded for your own self-assuredness?

During one of our many family trips to Delhi, my parents took us kids to see the India Gate, a towering arch-shaped war memorial. After viewing it up-close, my brother and I explored the lush lawns surrounding the imposing structure. We found large, rectangular trenches in the ground and my brother suggested we play games in there. I stared at the bright green in the trench.

"Are you sure that's grass?" I asked.

But egged on by others, my brother had already jumped over the ledge and landed waist deep in water. My mother chided him as she cleaned the green algae off him. It was a lesson in confidence, hubris, and the fine line between.

(RE)DEFINING CONFIDENCE

So, how confident are you? No, really, have you ever been asked that? Are you the type of person that hesitates or dives right in?

Confidence is defined as a *feeling of self-assurance arising from one's appreciation of one's own abilities.* Now, from an evolutionary standpoint, I think one could say that men generally had to be confident in their belief that they could kill that large beast. In other words, confidence in their projected ability often fueled their action. Women, on the other hand, were perhaps mastering many skills, driving themselves to be better and better at them. Once they received external validation from their peers, matriarch, or leader, they perhaps felt confident to be able to appreciate their own abilities. What drove them to feel confident was often a sense of mastery after having actually executed the task.

There is no right or wrong in the blustery, bravado associated with men or the tentative, self-doubt felt by many women. This is not men versus women; this is not good or bad. It was a matter of survival, as the survival of our very species depended on it! But fast-forward to the present day: Is it possible, given this evolutionary construct, with seemingly unknown parameters, that self-doubt comes rushing to us because we have never slayed that beast before? This, while men display the propensity to be over-confident, hence the emergence of the so-called "confidence gap"?[68]

MEN, WOMEN, AND CONFIDENCE

Within organizational management and psychology, the role confidence plays in one's career trajectory became a focal point, particularly how it may differ for women and men. One study found that men tend to overestimate their abilities and performance[69] while women underestimate both, *even though the quality of their performance does not differ*. Experts think this translates to a gap in confidence, presumably associated with lack of action, which may hamper professional advancement of women. In light of the small number of women in leadership roles, these findings have led to many self-help game plans that have been proposed to encourage women to project more confidence.

But there are two sides to every story. The "confidence gap" theory has also been challenged. Recent studies have shown that women in today's achievement-oriented organizations regard themselves as just as capable as men. One study found that appearing self-confident did not translate into influence equally for men and women.[70] Moreover, women's self-reported confidence in being at top of their game also did not correlate with how others judged their confidence level.

Such a complex issue can't be attributed to a single factor, nor can a single study alone provide a comprehensive understanding of the gender biases at play, while at work.

MINDING THE GAP

Women inventors hold a small share of patents, specifically in engineering fields.[71] At the current rate of progress, gender equity is estimated to be more than 75 years away. As someone who holds patents, I can say with full confidence that my own journey has often been riddled with self-doubt. I had to develop tools to help combat these feelings. Even with these tools, I can attest to the feeling of anxiety that exists every time I embark on a new endeavor. I am transparent about it. This feeling is not to be misconstrued as a lack of confidence. On the contrary, the anxiety actually fuels me to gain enough knowledge to be extremely well prepared to handle challenges. Over the years I have learned that I am blessed with many strengths, and that many of my strengths can be my weaknesses. But I don't hide my strengths, and I don't hide from my weaknesses!

---

[68] Kay and Shipman, "The Confidence Gap," The Atlantic, May 2014.

[69] Stephen Johnson, "Study: Men significantly more likely to overestimate their own intelligence," Big Think, April 6, 2018.

[70] Laura Guillen, "Is the Confidence Gap Between Men and Women a Myth?" Harvard Business Review, March 26, 2018.

[71] World Intellectual Property Organization, "New WIP Figures Show Highest-Ever Rate of Women Inventors, but Gender Gap Persists," April 26, 2018.

The solution may not be rooted in, *Just learn how to be more confident*, so much as, *Learn how to manage these feelings when they emerge*. Minding the confidence gap for me has been more about mind over matter, but not the *Fake it 'till you make it* kind!

For those who find that they experience success-oriented confidence, it will be important to have multitude of diverse experiences which can stitch together a narrative of *I have done that before*. I believe it starts with action that gives us success and leads to confidence. On the other hand, for many men, it may start with confidence that leads to action and gives success. So, to feel confident, we must take action and do things, undergoing experiences that can make us more and more comfortable in our own abilities. I have been fortunate to be in a company like 3M with a strong culture of empowerment that facilitated my growth and development.

MIND GAMES

For example, in late 2017, I was sitting in Amsterdam's airport and I got a phone call offering me an additional role that didn't exist in the company nor in any other company I knew. My irrational inner voice surfaced like a well-honed muscle memory, triggered by years of practice, to unhelpfully inform me: *I don't think you can do it.*

Like an uninvited guest, this reflex invaded my mind in that moment before I could even register it. It stems from a vicious cycle, rooted in self-doubt, overthinking, and paralysis. All your abilities, all your qualifications give way to this one worry: *Can I do it?* Inevitably, that feeling will come for many of us. So, what did I do to manage it? I took a deep breath to calm myself down and had a chat with myself. (Good thing I was at the airport where nobody knew me!) The conversation went something like this:

Me: Well, they could have called anybody, right?

Also Me: Yeah?

Me: But they called you. So, they must think you can do it.

Also Me: Okay, that makes sense.

Me: Second question: Have you done a job before that didn't exist?

Also Me: Yeah, actually, I have.

Me: How did that work out for you?

Also Me: You know, it was really good!

Me: Have you ever taken on complex roles, broken it down, and forged a path where none existed?

Also Me: Yes, I have, I have done that.

Me: Have you reached out to people when you needed them, and have they helped you navigate difficult situations?

Also Me: Yeah, actually they have, it's kind of nice because...

Me: Okay, okay, we get it, we get it. And did you or did you not say that you want to be a trailblazer? Did you or did you not say that you wanted to be part of something bigger? That you wanted to be a role model for your daughter?

Also Me: Yes. Yes. Yes.

My virtuous cycle was predictable, it came right on time. It allowed me to embrace an incredible position: Chief Science Advocate. Thankfully, I didn't miss out on this opportunity simply because I hadn't done it before. No one had!

In looking back, my success hasn't emerged from fighting thousands of years of evolution, but in figuring out how to avoid the potentially vicious cycle of self-doubt and over-thinking. I share this because I want my hindsight to be foresight for all the bright young minds about to embark on their own journey. Early in my career, I didn't know that my sense of self-doubt, and lack of self-assuredness, could largely be the manifestation of an evolutionary trait unique to my gender. I didn't know that I was experiencing a general lack of what one typically calls "confidence", especially when compared to men. I was unaware that, perhaps, there are differences between the very definition of confidence, and how it is processed, projected, and perceived.

With age and experience I have discovered that this is my virtuous cycle: *Action, success, confidence!*

My journey has been one of *authenticity*, of figuring out what drives me and where my passion and purpose align. It has been about building my own brand of *confidence* and of developing *trust*, with others, myself, and my capabilities. For me, it has been about always taking *initiative*, big and small, to build that positive narrative in the head. It has been about learning to spot patterns and see *opportunity*, and finally, of building a strong *network* through diverse experiences and extensive collaboration. These elements, listed below, trigger the self-talk which promptly lead me to my virtuous cycle!

Authenticity

Confidence

Trust

Initiative

Opportunity

Network

It is important to take ACTION while staying positively charged. That, in itself, is a catalyst for confidence. After all, the same words spell CATION! We need to take ACTION because we need women, and for that matter all under-represented minorities, to have a seat at the table. The world needs to unlock the secrets to a sustainable future. No one monolithic group has a monopoly on good ideas, *however confident they may seem*. We need all the creative solutions and diversity of thought we can get. The way I see it, the survival of our species depends on it!

THE CONFIDENCE GAME: OF GAPS, EDGES, LEDGES, AND JUDGES

I've had many peers, male allies, and supportive managers at 3M who regularly provide me with constructive feedback and validation. Our culture makes me feel empowered to authentically project my style of confidence. I even find myself clearly stating outright when I am confident about something, which should be perceived as a true confidence edge!

It's evident that the very definition of confidence and how it is internalized by different people may be different. We need to have more diversity of thought to appreciate different styles, and not just related to gender but the many other vectors of diversity. Now begins the waiting game for women and other diverse candidates to achieve parity in leadership positions.

So, what's the next move in the confidence game? In my view:

- **Women and people who struggle with confidence:** *The name of the game is* to find your own virtuous cycle that allows you to stay authentic to who you are. Be sure to communicate how the way you function is not leading to inaction.

- **Men and people who feel confident:** *Closing the confidence gap isn't a zero-sum game,* we can all benefit from it. Understand that the typical male experience of outward confidence may not be the only indicator of talent or skills.

- **Managers and supervisors:** *Make it a fair game.* Do not expect all women to model to the entrenched male definition of confident style. There's a lot to lose if everybody thinks the same way! Make rewards, recognitions, and hiring processes transparent

- **Organizations and institutions:** *Think of the endgame:* a workplace that celebrates inclusivity in its many ways. Eliminate any unfair pay gaps that could exacerbate feelings of poor confidence. Make efforts to continue to educate on unconscious bias.

According to 3M SOSI (State of Science Index), 92% of the parents said they want their kids to know more about science. **Parents,** *a rule of the game*: Encourage your children equally when it comes to interest in science.

Also, among those surveyed, 43% of women and 50% of men regret not pursuing science. Whether it is hard-wiring, social conditioning, or other factors, I can't help but think of how many inventors, and inventions, we are missing out on because a large subset of the population experienced a "confidence gap". **Society** *should have skin in this game.*

POINTS TO PONDER

What struggles have you faced with "confidence" and how has it impacted you?

How have you helped yourself or someone else turn a confidence gap to a confidence edge?

One Simple Tip for
That "Work-Life Balance" Resolution!

The lines between work and life are blurred, more than ever. For many of us, work is such an integral part of our life that we work hard to have a sense of purpose, at *work*. Work and life certainly aren't at odds with each other as the two pans of a classic *balance* would imply.

So, what does work-life balance mean, anyway? Apparently, the term was first used to signify the importance of leisure time outside of work. Over the years, the focus shifted to somehow represent the compartmentalization of work-life and home-life. But, with the current state of technology, we can be connected to work while at home or almost anywhere for that matter. This can translate into more work time at home, which is typically associated with an increase in stress. Given that, there is compelling research and widespread acceptance of supporting flexibility to reduce stress and shift the work-life dynamic, which can help drive productivity and employee engagement.[72] So, the focus has shifted to more of a work-life *integration*, and rightfully so.

A simple tip: For a better work-life integration, and lower associated stress, acknowledge *work-life semblance!*

Now that work and life are so inextricably intertwined, can the similarities between work-life and home-life be embraced more to lower the stress related to each? Could the recognition, acceptance, and even the incorporation of the features at the heart of work-life semblance be the next frontier in the ever-evolving work-life story? Could it help facilitate not only employee engagement but more sustainable innovation, inspirational leadership, global effectiveness, and diversity and inclusion?

Does this bring the concept of work-life full circle? Life lived with work woven in as an element, a critical one at that.

At a high level, our home-life is typically so much more about:
- **Process** over outcomes
- **Trust** and **candid** conversations
- **Higher context** decision-making
- **Longer-term** focus

---

[72] Shoemaker, Brown, and Barbour, "A Revolutionary Change: Making the Workplace More Flexible," Solutions.

WORK PARLANCE

It seems that these very elements can, oftentimes, be at odds with our typical corporate work-life functioning. But embracing these concepts for work can help avoid the mental fatigue every time one has to seemingly switch from work-life mode to home-life mode. The more aligned the two are, the more natural and authentic it will perhaps feel, thereby, lowering stress. Much has also been said about authenticity and its positive impact in the workplace.[73]

Let's take job performance, a major source of work-life stress. Stress is compounded when the focus of complex projects at work is on the outcome and not necessarily on the effort. When an employee's worth is singularly tied to an outcome-based metric, there is strong likelihood that the outcome not only becomes the focus but deters one from exploring new and disruptive things due to the perceived sense of increased risk. Tying worth to outcome can be at odds with so much of what most of us aspire to do in our home-life. We try to put in our best effort, and that makes the process itself rewarding regardless of outcome, especially for complex and humbling tasks such as that of raising kids, being parents.

On the flip side, in the effort to prioritize projects, initiatives, or resources at work, we seemingly focus so much on the mechanics and structural processes that there is a distinct risk of losing the rich context and the potential narrative. Acceptance of work-life semblance may allow us to ascribe the right amount of importance to seeking, developing, and appreciating the context, holistically, before the actual decision-making, much like we do at home. This should have the added benefit of bringing the low-context and high-context cultures on the same page for directions or decisions that impact global teams.[74] (High-context cultures rely more on implicit communication and nonverbal cues with a great deal of background information while low-context cultures rely on explicit communication with more of the information being defined and spelled out.)

Another key example where we could benefit from work-life semblance is in striving to achieve the right balance for short-term versus long-term focus. It is prudent in our home-lives to be thinking about the future, but how often at work do we find ourselves faced with excessive focus on short-term results, at the expense of long-term outlook and interests?

TAKE HOME

Our home-life is certainly more in our direct control when compared to our work-life. It can be argued that home-lives are less multifaceted than work-lives at

---

[73]Vanessa Buote, "Why You Should Bring Your Authentic Self to Work," Ascend: Harvard Business Review, October 19.
[74]Erin Meyer, "Navigating the Cultural Minefield," Harvard Business Review, May 2014.

times, but still many parallels could be drawn for a more seamless integration. Just being mindful of this simple question could potentially help: *How would I do this, or how would I go about making this decision, if it were my home-life?*

Of course, it may not work for everyone. But I have personally benefitted from acceptance of work-life semblance, and it helped me stay truly authentic to who I am as a person, resulting in lower stress. It tied in my principles and values, the culture I was raised in, and my desire to be accepted for who I am, which to me was an important criterion for contentment and success. Allowing myself to be honest, transparent, and vulnerable helped me develop at a personal and professional level. It also helped me build deeper levels of trust and collaboration with my colleagues, as a result of more candid communications with management, peers, and my teams.

My company played a strong role in facilitating this journey, including adherence to McKnight Principles, developing the "15% Culture", and encouraging programs like the Genesis Grants that empower process over outcome for new and disruptive ideas. Our Tech Forum events, by the technical community and for the technical community, allow opportunity to build narrative and share context around our Technology Platforms. "Dual Ladder" allows technical people to have tremendous influence despite not being in people management. Above all, the inspiring brand platform: 3M Science. Applied to Life.™

It works both ways! We can all perhaps benefit from making home-life decisions with a little more discipline and work-life decisions with a little more heart?

POINTS TO PONDER

What elements of semblance have helped or can help you in your work-life?

What elements of home-life have helped you at work?

Graduation!
Of Thinking-Caps, Town-Gown
Relationships and Degrees of Difficulty...

Commencement season always evokes fond memories of this time from my child-hood. Our town would be abuzz with news of luminaries who would be visiting, and celebrities who would be performing, for the annual convocation festivities. This small town, in the foothills of the majestic Himalayas and on the banks of the mighty River Ganges Canal, had one of the most prestigious engineering schools in India, the oldest technical institution in all of Asia. The same town was also home to the Central Building Research Institute, the Irrigation Research Institute, *and* the Army Corp of Engineers. It seemed as if *everyone* in the community was a STEM professional, or, inspired or encouraged to be one. Many of us aspired to such careers without even understanding what these professions entailed.

SONG IN YOUR HEART

I had a keen interest in poetry, and an early clue came from our institute's *kulgeet*. *Kul* means family and *geet* means song in Hindi; so, it literally translates to the *"family song"* of our hometown technical institute. Three concepts in particular stood out to me. They roughly translate to...

- Bring in a **new era**...new ideas, new dreams, new inspiration...
- Commit to the **greater good**, the good of the people...
- Nothing big will be achieved without **hard work!**

If you think about it, those lines are universal, not just applicable to STEM educa-tion, and they are more inspirational than anything. Even though I didn't study in my hometown institute, these words in many ways have guided my educational journey in India, and later, in the United States. I feel fortunate to live them every day through my work at 3M and even life outside of work.

FIGURE OF SPEECH

The significance of these was validated through findings of the 2019 3M SOSI. The world wants solutions to some big challenges we face as humanity. The public feels disconnected with the experts and considers them elitist. Yet, the global community is counting on the expertise and our ability to work hard collectively to solve challenging problems. So, the words I tell freshly minted graduates, with their caps, gowns and degrees, I also share with you. As you ready yourself for the next phase of your journey, here are few things to remember:

- **Keep your thinking-cap on!**

  The world needs new ideas and creative solutions to the challenges we face. Never stop learning. Seek diverse perspectives. Be engaged. Be present. Be mindful. Bring a new energy and vision in whatever you do, wherever you go. Hold on to that energy and enthusiasm you feel today, inspiring yourself and others around you with your passion and innovative ideas. I have been fortunate to be able to live by this principle and usher in new ideas, empowered by a culture of innovation.

- **The town and gown relationship is critical.**

  I am not referring to the historically strained relationships when colleges literally walled themselves from the surrounding communities. I am using it in a broader sense to identify the relationship between the highly educated and the general public. A chasm between the two hurts us all in the long run. A commitment to the greater good will keep a focus on people and community in the forefront. In turn, the people and community will inspire our endeavors; they certainly did inspire me.

- **Most worthy endeavors have a higher degree of difficulty.**

  And I hope you all take many of these on and leave a legacy. These will require grit, determination, and plain hard work. It will require hard choices and sacrifices. You will have to push and you will have to persist to make your vision a reality. Inspire others to join you, collaborate, and cooperate; challenges will seem more surmountable, less difficult. I feel fortunate to have the support to take on challenging initiatives, and I know that many worthy causes await champions, like you.

POINTS TO PONDER

*What advice would you give to fresh
STEM graduates based on your experience?*

*What opportunities do you see to connect
STEM initiatives with public need?*

Making the List?
Of Footprints, Fingerprints, and Imprints...

List-making can be a very ceremonious activity at the end of summer in many households. But lists took on a new significance during the back-to-school season in 2019 when *Forbes* published a list highlighting America's Most Innovative Leaders.[75] If the central idea was truly intended to hail ***innovation*** or ***leadership***, the criteria used seemed outdated at best.

THE HIT (OR-MISS) LIST

This list of 100 of the most "Innovative Leaders in America" had 99 men on it (and one woman). You didn't have to be a woman to shake your head or roll your eyes at this list. Being a reasonable human being would just about do it. It seemed that "innovative" signified only market cap dollars and "leader" was essentially a CEO. So, it was no surprise that many organizations, groups, and individuals responded with scathing commentary. Several even took it upon themselves to publish their own lists in light of what Rita J. King dubbed, the "lazy list". It was quite the weekend of off-the-charts uproar.[77] By Sunday, the editor had posted a response, admitting the methodology was "flawed".[78]

As Moira Forbes, the first woman from the Forbes family to be part of the company, pointed out, "Rather than spotlighting the most dynamic minds in business, [the list] perpetuated damaging and misleading stereotypes." She went on to say that the criteria used to generate the list essentially favored the CEOs of the largest public companies, where women's presence remains "woefully anemic".[79]

The list was a lost opportunity to crystallize what it means to be innovative, and to catalyze a conversation towards progress with criteria that strongly favor a balanced approach to leadership. It was only a month preceding this controversy, a diverse roster of CEOs had signed the Statement on the Purpose of a Corporation that I talked about earlier which should spell the end of the days of "Business is business, and the

[75]"America's Most Innovative Leaders," Forbes, September 3, 2019.
[76]Rita J. King, "99 Problems: Forbes 'Most Innovative'," LinkedIn, September 7, 2019.
[77]Jena McGregor, "'We blew it': Forbes named 99 men and only one woman on its list of 'most innovative leaders'," The Washington Post, September 10, 2019.
[78]Randall Lane, "Opportunity Missed: Reflecting On The Lack of Women On Our Most Innovative Leaders List," Forbes, September 8, 2019.
[79]Moira Forbes, "Where Were The Women On Forbes' Most Innovative Leaders List? We Can Do Better And We Will," Forbes, September 9, 2019.

sole focus of the CEO is to maximize the profits of that business." [80]

The lists and the aftermath calls for a necessary discussion on the revision of criteria for what it takes to be an innovative leader, including who sets the criteria, or should I say, the list of critical elements essential for defining innovation or leadership. The need for data, and the rigor of the process, often become convenient scapegoats to ignore the necessary shifts. As Rita J. King points out,

> *"...If a list of innovators doesn't start by focusing on the constraints shaping the practice, it's not worth the time it takes to read it. Any list of innovators should prioritize those who attempt to create a balanced approach to profits and humanity. Let's celebrate the avant-garde and get real about the role of business innovation in the modern world."*[76]

I agree that the methodology did not match the stated intent of the list. Criteria for celebrating innovative leadership needs to reflect the *heart* of what innovation means.

THE LIST-OFF

I had some list-worthy moments of my own the month Forbes published its list. Do-Something Strategic listed 50 amazing, dynamic, innovative women leading businesses and initiatives across the country, with the preamble: "Dynamism knows no gender, value creation is more than just money and innovation can come from anywhere." I was honored to be on this list with a few additional mentions as a result.

Être Magazine's new book Être: *Girls, Who Do You Want to Be?* became Amazon's #1 New Release in Self-Esteem for Teens & Young Adults on the first day of pre-orders! I was honored to be among the luminaries quoted and listed in this book.

And the most humbling moment was making it into the prestigious Carlton Society, or what is known as the 3M Hall of Fame. To be inducted as a member, one must do several things: One must develop new technology, have a major business impact, enhance 3M's reputation, and maintain the highest standards of integrity. On top of this, one must successfully mentor and inspire future generations of scientists. These criteria clearly focus on multiple stakeholders. It takes more than revenue for a person to make it on the list. The Carlton Society was ahead of its times, just like the visionary 3Mer Richard Carlton for whom the award is named. His legacy of innovation, and William McKnight's legacy of employee empowerment, have had a profound impact on our company culture and my own career. I was honored to be the fourth woman on this list and the first woman engineer to ever be inducted!

---

[80] "Business Roundtable Redefines the Purpose of a Corporation to Promote 'An Economy That Serves All Americans'," Business Roundtable, August 19, 2020.

THE WISH-LIST

Diversity, inclusion, and recognition matter. The 3M CEO has signed on to the statement of purpose that specifically focuses on fostering diversity and inclusion, dignity and respect. The critics of stakeholder capitalism argue that any purpose other than shareholder profits results in a lack of focus, but it is great to see corporations and CEOs expanding their focus. The same should happen with recognition; the criteria needs to evolve.

Making the list should be about more than *printing* money. In my view, it should also be about the indelible marks one leaves in the process: where you go, what you do, and how you do it.

- **Footprints** represent the *path* and the *milestones.*
  It's about blazing new trails, charting the course, and pushing the envelope, as hard as it may seem. Oftentimes, it's about moving the needle to eventually move mountains, as I like to say it. It is about forging a path where none existed and creating a lasting legacy with a journey of authenticity, passion, and purpose. The goal is to improve lives. I will forever remember that September Week of Lists as a milestone marking some of the ways I have been able to make an impact by breaking down barriers, biases, and boundaries along the way.

- **Fingerprints** represent the *work* and the *results.*
  It's about the handiwork in architecting a vision and hands-on work to execute for impact. It's about the leadership demonstrated and influence exerted that profoundly changes not just the innovation, but impacts the processes, the people, the culture, and the very DNA itself. It is the collaborating seamlessly across functions, boundaries and silos to deliver meaningful results. I am inspired to continue to identify problems to solve and continue working with amazing people to push the limits of what is possible and make lives easier with our technology, products, and innovation.

- **Imprints** represent the impact on *minds* and *hearts.*
  It's about the human element, which includes the mentoring and coaching, as well as building bridges and alliances. It requires empathy and empowerment. Imprints are the elements of a legacy that inspire others with enthusiasm, while role-modeling the commitment and excitement that increases engagement with all stakeholders. Making the lists further reaffirms my commitment to advocacy, sharing my passion with others while mentoring the next generation to help them achieve their goals.

For those who got schooled on list making, it is important to remember that the rubrics matter, the metrics make a difference, and the optics have an impact. Our journey is just that, a journey, not a lonely march to a predetermined destination. It doesn't require a preset agenda with a preplanned prize. The early years may often seem meandering, but they are formative and to be enriched by education, exposure, and experiences. Oftentimes, as in my case, it was about lessons I didn't even know I learnt but could count on later in my journey.

The next phase is the road to discovery, where you essentially learn more about yourself. It's about figuring out not just what makes you tick but what holds you back. It is also about the beliefs that allow you to break through and eventually transition on to the path of enlightenment. This is when you want to share what you have learned about charting the course on your journey and feel rewarded by helping to engineer the future for those who are to come. This has been the heart of my science journey.

Full circle, with footprints, fingerprints, and imprints.

POINTS TO PONDER

What is at the heart of your science journey?

What footprints, fingerprints, and imprints would you like to leave?

"Science is no substitute for virtue; the heart is as necessary for a good life as the head."

— Bertrand Russell, British Philosopher and Polymath

ACKNOWLEDGMENTS

To my family. My parents, who always instilled the value of education and the mantra of simple living and high thinking in us. My father is a trail-blazing engineer in his own right, and the reason both my brother and I are engineers. My visionary mother always quoted lines, inspiring us to work hard, not to reach a destination but to forge a path even where none exists. My brother, attempts at competing with him as a kid, made me push myself harder. They all continue to encourage and guide me.

To my incredible husband, Raghu. Without his love, support, and wisdom I wouldn't be where I am today. He is my sounding board. My kids Aadarsh and Manashree, or should I say, freshly minted adults who keep my thinking fresh. They inspire me.

To all my gurus and my extended family and friends, spread over many continents, who have been cheerleaders for me along the way.

And, of course, everyone at 3M, and the extended SOSI team.

Thanks to the Society of Women Engineers (SWE) for the opportunity to publish this book, and the David James Group and my editor, Eli Trybula, for guidance and insightful discussions to bring the contents together.

BIBLIOGRAPHY

Aines, R.D. and Aines, A.L., *Championing Science: Communicating Your Ideas to Decision Makers,* Oakland, University of California Press, 2019.

"America's Most Innovative Leaders," *Forbes,* September 3, 2019.

Arya, A., "I'm a doctor in Minneapolis treating coronavirus patients. Until racism is abolished, it will always be a greater threat to justice than this virus," *Business Insider,* June 4, 2020.

Bailey, Z.D. et al., 2017. "Structural racism and health inequities in the USA: evidence and interventions," *The Lancet,* 389(10077): 1453-1463.

Bian, L., Leslie, S.J., and Cimpian, A., 2017. "Gender stereotypes about intellectual ability emerge early and influence children's interests," *Science,* 335(6323): 389-391.

Blacker, K., "Science of Adolescent Learning: Debunking the Myth about Left-Brain/Right-Brain Learning Styles," *Alliance for Excellent Education,* December 14, 2016.

Bongard, M., Ferrandez, J.M., and Fernandez, E., 2009. "The neural concert of vision," *Neurocomputing,* 72(4-6), 814-819.

Boucher, K.L. et al., 2017. "Can I work with and Help Others in This Field? How Communal Goals Influence Interest and Participation in STEM Fields," *Frontiers in Psychology,* 8(901):1-12.

Brower, T., "Onboarding During The Pandemic: How to Give New Employees A Running Start," *Forbes,* July 12, 2020.

Buote, V., "Why You Should Bring Your Authentic Self to Work," *Ascend: Harvard Business Review,* October 19.

"Business Roundtable Redefines the Purpose of a Corporation to Promote 'An Economy That Serves All Americans'," *Business Roundtable,* August 19, 2020.

Bustamante, A.S. and Hirsh-Pasek, K., "Learning about learning: Meaning matters," *Brookings Institution,* May 30, 2018.

Chugh, D., *The Person You Mean to Be*: How Good People Fight Bias, New York, HarperCollins Publishers, 2018.

Diekman, A.B. and Steinberg, M., 2013. "Navigating Social Roles in Pursuit of Important Goals: A Communal Goal Congruity Account of STEM Pursuits," *Social and Personality Psychology Compass,* 7: 487-501.

Degges-White, S., "Leading from the Heart," *Psychology Today,* February 5, 2015.

Epstein, D., *Range: Why Generalists Triumph in a Specialized World*, New York, Riverhead Books, 2019.

Forbes, M., "Where Were The Women On Forbes' Most Innovative Leaders List? We Can Do Better And We Will," *Forbes,* September 9, 2019.

Fore, H., "Don't let children be the hidden victims of COVID-19 pandemic," *UNICEF,* April 9, 2020.

Frank, R.H., "Why Luck Matters More Thank You Might Think," *The Atlantic,* May 2016.

Fraser-Thill, R., "Parent Involvement Can Benefit Children in Many Ways," *verywell family,* May 14, 2020.

George, B., "VUCA 2.0: A Strategy for Steady Leadership in an Unsteady World," *Forbes,* February 17, 2017.

Govindarajan, V. and Srinivas, S., "The Innovation Mindset in Action: 3M Corporation," *Harvard Business Review,* August 6, 2013.

Grant, A., "Why White People Stay Silent on Racism, and What to Read First," *Microsoft News,* June 7, 2020.

Gray, D.L. et al., 2020. "Engaging Black and Latinx students through communal learning opportunities: A relevance intervention for middle schoolers in STEM elective classrooms," *Contemporary Educational Psychology,* 60: 101833.

Guillen, L., "Is the Confidence Gap Between Men and Women a Myth?" *Harvard Business Review,* March 26, 2018.

Harter, J. and Adkins, A., "Employees Want a Lot More From Their Managers," *Gallup,* April 8, 2015.

Hicks, M., "Why tech's gender problem is nothing new," *The Guardian,* October 12, 2018.

Horgan, J., "Why STEM Students Need Humanities Courses," *Scientific American,* August 16, 2018.

Hughes, N.C., "1149: Daniel Burrus, Managing Uncertainty Caused by COVID-19," *The Tech Blog Writer*, March 22, 2020.

Johnson, S., "Study: Men significantly more likely to overestimate their own intelligence," *Big Think*, April 6, 2018.

Kahan, D.M. et al., 2017. "Science Curiosity and Political Information Processing," *Political Psychology*, 38: 179-199.

Kay, K. and Shipman, C., "The Confidence Gap," *The Atlantic*, May 2014.

Keating, C., *"Hidden Figures'* Real-life NASA Mathematician Katherine Johnson: 'If You Like What You're Doing, You Will Do Well'," *People,* January 29, 2017.

King, R.J., "99 Problems: Forbes 'Most Innovative'," *LinkedIn*, September 7, 2019.

Lane, R., "Opportunity Missed: Reflecting On The Lack of Women On Our Most Innovative Leaders List," *Forbes*, September 8, 2019.

Livni, E., "To thrive in a 'wicked' world, you need range," *Quartz*, June 9, 2019.

MH&L Staff, "What's the Secret of Companies Able to Pivot Supply Chains During Pandemic?" *Material Handling & Logistics*, April 28, 2020.

McGrane, C., "Misconceptions and stereotypes may discourage girls from studying STEM, study finds," *GeekWire*, March 13, 2018.

McGregor, J., "'We blew it': Forbes named 99 men and only one woman on its list of 'most innovative leaders'," *The Washington Post*, September 10, 2019.

Meyer, E., "Navigating the Cultural Minefield," *Harvard Business Review*, May 2014.

Mooney, C., "The Science of Why We Don't Believe Science," Mother Jones, May/June 2011.

Morgan Roberts, L. and Washington, E.F., "U.S. Businesses Must Take Meaningful Action Against Racism," *Harvard Business Review*, June 1, 2020.

National Science Foundation, National Center for Science and Engineering Statistics, 2019. "Women, Minorities, and Persons with Disabilities in Science and Engineering: 2019." Special Report NSF 19-304.

Neela-Stock, S., "Scientists strike to call out systemic racism in STEM," *Mashable*. June 10, 2020.

"Nobel Prize Inspiration Initiative," *The Nobel Prize* accessed in May, 2018 at https://www.nobelprize.org/nobel-prize-inspiration-initiative/.

O'Connor, S., "The Secret Power of Play," *Time Magazine*, September 6, 2017.

Omens, A., "How To Be A Stakeholder-Driven Company In A Pandemic," *Forbes*, March 12, 2020.

Pierce, D., "Five ways to build a community of learners online," *eSchool News*, June 11, 2020.

Quinn, D.M. and Polikoff, M., "Summer learning loss: What is it, and what can we do about it?" *Brookings Institution*, September 14, 2017.

Radjou, N., Prabhu, J., and Ahuja, S., *Jugaad Innovation: Think Frugal, Be Flexible, Generate Breakthough Growth*, San Francisco, Jossey-Bass, 2012.

Seth, D., "Medicine vs. racism: White coats for Black lives," *KevinMD*. June 3, 2020.

Shoemaker, J., Brown, A., and Barbour, R., 2011. "A Revolutionary Change: Making the Workplace More Flexible," *Solutions*, 2(2): 52-62.

Shmerling, R.H., "Right brain/left brain, right?" *Harvard Health Blog*, August 25, 2017.

Stone, E., "The Emerging Science of Awe and Its Benefits," *Psychology Today*, April 27, 2017.

Travers, M., "Were People Worried About a Pandemic Before COVID-19? Hardly, According to a Study of Global Attitudes," *Forbes*, March 24, 2020.

U.N. News, "Ahead of International Day of Women and Girls in Science, UN calls for smashing stereotypes," February 9, 2018.

Wakeman, C., "How I'm Committing To Evolve," *Reality Based Leadership*, June 4, 2020.

World Intellectual Property Organization, "New WIP Figures Show Highest-Ever Rate of Women Inventors, but Gender Gap Persists," April 26, 2018.

Zambrano, J., Garam A.L., Leal, C.C., and Thoman, D.B., 2020. "Highlighting Prosocial Affordances of Science in Textbooks to Promote Science Interest." *CBE – Life Sciences Education*, 19(3), ar24.

ABOUT THE AUTHOR

Jayshree Seth, Ph.D., is a Corporate Scientist for 3M Company, headquartered in St. Paul, Minnesota, USA, where she has worked for over 27 years. She holds 70 patents on a variety of innovations, with several others pending. Dr. Seth uses scientific knowledge, technical expertise, and professional experience to advance science and develop new products. She currently leads applied technology development for sustainable industrial products in 3M's Industrial Adhesives and Tapes Division. She is also 3M's first-ever Chief Science Advocate and is charged with communicating the importance of science in everyday life, breaking down barriers, and building excitement around STEM careers. She is very passionate about teaching, coaching, mentoring and is a sought-after speaker, globally, on a multitude of topics such as innovation, leadership, and science advocacy. Dr. Seth has been interviewed in national and international media, and she has featured in 3M brand campaigns and commercials.

Dr. Seth is the fourth woman and first woman engineer to attain the highest technical designation of Corporate Scientist at 3M, as well as induction into the 3M Carlton Society, which honors the very best among the scientific community. She is also a certified Design for Six Sigma Black Belt. At 3M, she has served on the CEO Inclusion Council, chaired the Asian and Asian American Employee Network (A3CTION), and serves on the Women's Leadership Forum (WLF) Technical Chapter. She has received numerous 3M excellence awards and a record-setting number of intrapreneurial grants to drive innovation. She was conferred the 2020 Achievement Award from the Society of Women Engineers (SWE), the 2019 International Women & Technologies' Le Tecnovisionarie® award for sustainability, the 2020 Woman of Distinction by Girl Scouts River Valley, the 2018 Distinguished Alumni Award from her alma mater in India, and was also among engineers selected to attend the National Academy of Engineering's (NAE) 14th annual U.S. Frontiers of Engineering symposium.

Dr. Seth grew up in Northern India, in the university town of Roorkee, at the foothills of the Himalayas and on the banks of the River Ganges canal. She holds a B.Tech. in chemical engineering from NIT, Trichy, India, and an M.S. and Ph.D. in chemical engineering from Clarkson University, New York. Jayshree is a member of the Engineering Advisory Council for Clarkson University. Dr. Seth has over 15 journal publications based on her graduate work, co-authoring several with her husband, who also works at 3M. They enjoy extending science, creativity, and innovation into their kitchen. They have two adult children. Dr. Seth enjoys experiencing other cultures and she is also an avid reader, writer and poet.

Dr. Seth is active on social media.
You can follow her on LinkedIn, Twitter, and Instagram.
Twitter: @jseth2, Insta: sethjayshree

Made in the USA
Columbia, SC
10 September 2021